YO-CHC-934

# THE POOR

A CULTURE OF POVERTY, OR A POVERTY OF CULTURE?

# THE POOR

## A CULTURE OF POVERTY, OR A POVERTY OF CULTURE?

*Edited by*

**J. ALAN WINTER**
*Associate Professor of Sociology*
*Connecticut College*

*Foreword by*

Thomas W. Georges, Jr.

*Introduction by*

J. Alan Winter

*Essays and Comments by*

Nathan Glazer
Frederick D. Holliday
Charles V. Willie
Herbert Aptheker
Hylan Lewis
Arthur Shostak
Walter B. Miller
Elliot Liebow

**WILLIAM B. EERDMANS/PUBLISHER**
**Grand Rapids, Michigan**

Copyright © 1971 by William B. Eerdmans Publishing Company

All rights reserved

Library of Congress Catalog Card Number: 70-132032

Printed in the United States of America


The essay "The Culture of Poverty? What Does It Matter?"
by Hylan Lewis copyright © 1969 by Hylan Lewis.

*To Gail, Wendy and Miriam*

## LIST OF CONTRIBUTORS

Herbert Aptheker
> Director, American Institute for Marxist Studies and Visiting Lecturer, Bryn Mawr College.

Thomas W. Georges, Jr.
> Associate Vice-President of Community Health Services and Community Affairs, Temple University; formerly, Secretary, Department of Public Welfare, Commonwealth of Pennsylvania.

Nathan Glazer
> Professor of Education and Social Structure, Harvard University.

Frederick D. Holliday
> Principal, Simon Gratz High School, Philadelphia, Pennsylvania.

Hylan Lewis
> Professor of Sociology, Brooklyn College.

Elliot Liebow
> Chief, Special Project Section, Mental Health Study Center, NIMH.

Walter B. Miller
> Research Associate, Joint Center for Urban Studies of M.I.T. and Harvard University.

Arthur Shostak
> Professor of Social Science, Drexel University.

Charles V. Willie
> Professor and Chairman, Department of Sociology, Syracuse University.

J. Alan Winter
> Associate Professor of Sociology, Connecticut College.

# ACKNOWLEDGMENTS

The papers and comments presented herein were delivered as part of the Conference on the Culture of Poverty held at Temple University of the Commonwealth System of Higher Education on October 10 and 11, 1969. I was co-ordinator of the conference and was, at that time, on the Temple University faculty. The conference was made possible by funds from Temple University and the National Institute of Mental Health (Grant MN 08578-06). Special thanks are due to: David Austin, Robert J. Kleiner, William Phillips, Leonard Savitz and Holgar Stub for their part in planning the conference; Ruth Horowitz, Gail Schmuckler and Paul Vitt for their help with the myriad administrative details associated with the conference; Harry A. Bailey and Leon Ovsiew each of whom served excellently as the moderator of panel discussions held as part of the conference; and, of course, to the speakers themselves. Special thanks are also due to Bernadette Barattini who typed the first draft and to Doreen V. Desmangles who typed the final draft of the manuscript.

—**J. A. W.**

*Philadelphia, Pa.*

# CONTENTS

# FOREWORD

To discuss the culture of poverty in the United States is to discuss the culture of hell, for it is hell on earth to be poor in the United States of America. This hell is populated by outcasts who are systematically and routinely punished by systems that make escape almost impossible—systems whose task, year after year, is to devise more and more complicated mazes, labeled "exit," but usually leading nowhere; systems that present solutions to poverty that help the non-poor more than the poor; systems that close off the escape routes from the culture of hell and then criticize the poor for remaining poor.

With all its riches and resources America is for many Americans a land of paradox. America will probably be the last of the western industrial nations where lack of money and lack of earning power will condemn people to hell on earth.

While poverty itself is poorness—lack of money—we all recognize that poverty is also composed of chronic unemployment and underemployment, urban and rural slum environment, little education, broken families and poor physical and mental health. Let us look at some of those component parts of poverty to see whether we are dealing with them honestly or adding to the national tradition of paradox and hoax.

National tradition of paradox and hoax? Let us document that a little bit.

1. Quote from American History: "Christopher Columbus discovered America in 1492."
   FACT: The Indians were already there.
2. The Declaration of Independence (July 4, 1776) declared, among other things, "that all men are created equal, that they are endowed with certain inalienable Rights by their Creator, that among these are life, liberty and the pursuit of happiness."
   FACT: In spite of these shining words, slavery was written into the Constitution of the United States.
3. The Declaration of Independence also stated "that to secure these rights [life, liberty, and the pursuit of happiness], Governments are instituted. Whenever any Form of Government becomes destructive to these ends, it is the right of the people to alter or to abolish it, and to institute a new Government. . . ."
   FACT: You try it.
4. In the latter half of the 19th century the United States "won the west."
   FACT: Americans were very nearly successful in their attempts to exterminate the Indian and the buffalo, who now are to be found in a state of captivity on reservations and in zoos, respectively.
   NOTE: Currently we read in the news media of a great American concern for the well-being of wildlife in the black nations of Africa. I do not read of any national American concern for human life in Rhodesia, the Union of South Africa or the Protectorate of Southwest Africa, or, indeed, for the American Indian.

Consider how America deals with problems of poverty.

Everyone agrees that unemployment and underemployment are part of the poverty complex. Unfortunately, there seems to be very little agreement on how much unemployment or underemployment exists and what, if anything, to do about it. Official Labor Department reports of unemployment grossly underestimate the shockingly high, real unemployment in the ghettos and barrios of America. It is clear that even our reporting systems are inappropriate when considering the needs of the poor. I believe that slum unemployment is as high as 15 to 20%. Underemployment is an everyday fact for the low income worker.

The wise economists in Washington say: "We are in an inflationary period. A little more unemployment would be a healthy way to cool the economy." The Congress of the United States in concert with the several Departments of the executive branch of government has made available 28 separate manpower training and placement programs, but none has been significantly effective.

Poverty is closely associated with relatively low levels of education. Unemployment rates are higher for people with little education. Conversely, completion of high school correlates with employment success. Poor children usually go to poor schools. Schools in low income neighborhoods are usually more poorly staffed, more poorly equipped and more poorly supplied with teaching materials. These poor schools furnish the child with little incentive, encouragement, or opportunity to finish high school and go on to college. In fact, many teen-agers feel pushed out of school.

Poor housing and poor neighborhoods are part of the culture of poverty. More than half of the housing occupied by low income families in the country is inadequate, dilapidated, and deteriorating. Not only is slum housing substandard—it is overpriced and overcrowded.

13

While some Americans have game rooms, poor children have the streets. They have the streets with filth, violence, alcohol, drugs, and other hazards of their substitutes for middle America's golf links, tennis courts, handball courts and swim clubs. Public housing projects are inadequate in number and concept and most are highly racist in operation. They are little more than warehouses where poor people are stored by race—but only if they qualify. The family cannot be too large: we do not build units for large families. Income limits make certain that the public housing projects bring together a large number of poor families to create a new kind of slum.

Although we need millions of housing units for low income families, public funds have constructed only 800,000 units in 31 years. In the past 34 years, tax monies have financed ten million housing units for middle and upper income families.

No consideration of the culture of poverty in America would be complete without noting urban renewal, an effective program of Negro removal that destroys substandard housing, forcing the occupants to move into other substandard dwellings, and then uses the sites to build commercial and luxury facilities.

Family disruption is highly prevalent in our society. Those with means can ease the trauma of family breakup through appropriate legal action and financial settlements. I believe that poverty itself is the leading cause of broken families among the poor and the financial problems are intensified with family breakup. Added to poverty, of course, is the lack of legal service to secure a divorce.

The large families among the poor bother some people a great deal. The size of poor Indian families has inspired American foundations and voluntary agencies to send birth control teams to India. The size of poor black and Spanish-American families is inspiring white middle-American voluntary agencies to open family planning clinics in the ghettos and barrios of America. The rationale commonly used is that the world population will outgrow the world food supply. Therefore, something must be done about the population explosion.

If that were the honest cause for concern, why not increase the world's food supply? Our national policy is to limit agricultural production, even to the extent of paying farmers not to grow crops on their lands. In addition, we employ a parity system to help keep food prices artificially high. At the same time, we use a food stamp program to expand the food purchasing power of the poor. It all adds up to another complex constellation whose prime beneficiary is the rich, not the poor.

Large families seem to be a characteristic of the poor and the very rich. If our concern centers around world population and food supply, it will be increasingly important to protect equitably the right of each family to make its own choices on the basis of what is best for the family.

Poor health is a part of the culture of poverty and a result of poverty. Poor housing, poor neighborhoods, crowding, poor education, lack of available and accessible health care, poor nutrition, inadequate income are all contributing factors. Poor people die younger, have more days of disability and sickness and lose more of their babies to death during the first year of life. Mental illness is endemic in poverty, but this correlation seems poorly understood.

Now, let us go back to the lack of money. Poverty is lack of money and lack of earning power associated with a host of other factors, including the ones already mentioned. In our society—our free enterprise, devil-take-the-hindmost, dollar-based society—there is no substitute for money. Poverty will be cured only by massive injections of money—directly to the poor.

15

In the last several years, the seeds of change have been planted in the hell that is the poor man's America, the black man's America, the Spanish-American's America. Television is showing everyone what the American Dream is like: we all see the comfortable homes, the nice clothing, the good meals, the classrooms, the luxury, the clean streets, the courteous policemen. I hope this book will help those who wish to actively explore ways to give everyone a chance to live the American Dream. I am convinced that there is a way of erasing the American paradox and hoax: a way of making the American Dream come true. America must consciously, deliberately, and rationally create a society that eliminates poverty.

Remember, if the Dream is to be American, it must be for everyone.

—Thomas W. Georges, Jr.

# INTRODUCTION: THE CULTURE OF POVERTY HYPOTHESES AND THEIR IMPORT FOR SOCIAL SCIENCE AND SOCIAL POLICY

## J. ALAN WINTER

The essays in this volume and the comments on them were originally prepared for a conference on the import for social science and social policy of Oscar Lewis' treatment of the culture of poverty. In order to provide the reader with a proper background for understanding the context in which these papers were written, it is necessary to summarize Lewis' discussions of the culture of poverty.[1] I believe his discussions can best be understood as offering three related hypotheses concerning the poor. These hypotheses are: (1) that the way of life of the poor in many nations comprises a relatively unique configuration of behavioral patterns

[1] See Oscar Lewis, *Five Families: Mexican Case Studies in the Culture of Poverty* (New York: Basic Books, 1959); *Tepozlan: Village in Mexico* (New York: Holt, 1960); *The Children of Sanchez* (New York: Random House, 1961); *Pedro Martinez* (New York: Random House, 1964); "The Culture of Poverty," *Scientific American*, CCXV, No. 4 (Oct. 1966), 19-25; *La Vida: A Puerto Rican Family in the Culture of Poverty — San Juan and New York* (New York: Random House, 1966).

17

and values; (2) that this configuration constitutes a true culture or subculture and not a mere set of transient adaptations to objective conditions; and (3) that this configuration is most likely to appear among the poor in a class-stratified, highly individualized capitalistic society. The configurations of behaviors and values in question are what Lewis refers to as the "culture of poverty."

This introductory essay will consist of three main sections. Each of the sections will first discuss one of Lewis' hypotheses and then turn to the views of the contributors to this volume bearing on that hypothesis. These latter discussions will focus on criticisms of Lewis' views, since the consensus among the contributors was highly critical of his views. Two judgments lay behind their criticism. First, there was the conclusion that Lewis' treatment of the culture of poverty was not likely to advance social scientific understanding of the nature of poverty and the lives of the poor. Second, there was a common fear that the "culture of poverty" concept might well have several unintended, but nonetheless very negative, consequences.

## I. THE CONTENT OF THE CULTURE OF POVERTY

### a. Lewis' Hypothesis

In all, Lewis lists over seventy characteristics of what he calls the "culture of poverty." His list must be regarded as hypothetical since it is possible that the poor do not have a distinctive way of life or, if they do, that it is characterized by few, if any, of the traits he lists. The final status of Lewis' hypothesized list and a more definitive description of the life-ways of the poor await further research.

The seventy-odd traits that Lewis lists are grouped by him into four major categories: relationships between the subculture and the larger society; the nature of the local slum community; the nature of the family; and the attitudes, values and character of the individual. Thus, he contends:

> 1. The lack of effective participation and integration of the poor in the major institutions of the larger society is one of the crucial characteristics of the culture of poverty.[2]
>
> 2. When we look at the culture of poverty on the local community level, we find ... above all a minimum of organization beyond the level of the nuclear and extended family.[3]
>
> 3. On the family level the major traits of the culture of poverty are the absence of childhood as a specially prolonged and protected stage in the life cycle, early initiation into sex, free unions or consensual marriages, a relatively high incidence of abandonment of wives and children, a trend toward female- or mother-centered families, ... a strong predisposition toward authoritarianism, lack of privacy, ... and competition for limited goods and maternal affection.[4]
>
> 4. On the level of the individual the major characteristics are a strong feeling of marginality, of helplessness, or of dependence and inferiority.[5]

In addition, Lewis notes that "other traits include a high incidence of ... weak ego structure, confusion of sexual identification, a lack of impulse control, ... little ability to defer gratification and to plan for the future, a sense of resignation and fatalism. ..."[6] Finally, he notes,

> People with a culture of poverty are provincial. ... They know only of their own troubles, their own local conditions, their own neighborhood, their own way of life

2 *La Vida,* p. xlv.
3 *Ibid.,* p. xlvi.
4 *Ibid.,* p. xlvii.
5 *Ibid.*
6 *Ibid.,* p. xlviii.

. . . . They are not class-conscious, although they are very sensitive indeed to status distinctions.[7]

### b. Social Scientific Criticisms

The basic criticism in these essays of Lewis' description of the so-called culture of poverty is, to put it simply, that it accentuates the negative and eliminates the positive. That is, Lewis is criticized for stressing the weaknesses in the "culture" and for ignoring its strengths. Charles V. Willie, for example, suggests that Lewis' description ignores the ability of at least the black poor in America to endure and transcend their poverty. Walter B. Miller enumerates and details four specific tendencies that, he suggests, lead Lewis to overemphasize the negative aspects of the culture of poverty. These tendencies are: (1) simple derogation, as in characterizing the culture of poverty as entailing a "poverty of culture" and the men in it as "irresponsible" and "generally unreliable"; (2) the use of hidden reference standards, usually the idealized practices of middle class adults as, for example, in the citation of a "lack of privacy" or an "early initiation into sex"; (3) the use of analytic or theoretical systems, such as psychodynamic theory, to judge the poor as, for example, having "weak ego structures" or "confusion of sex identity"; and (4) speculations as to subjective states of individuals, as in the claims that persons in the culture of poverty feel inferior or helpless. These four tendencies render Lewis' description of the so-called culture of poverty somewhat more negative than a more neutral or less theoretically committed observer might see it.

### c. Possible Negative Consequences

The pejorative character of much of Lewis' descrip-

[7] *Ibid.*

tion of the so-called culture of poverty is seen by contributors to this volume as threatening two unintended negative consequences. Both have something of the character of a "backlash" against Lewis' "findings." The first, referred to by Nathan Glazer, is the attempt by those sympathetic with the plight of the poor to deny the pejorative character of the description. As Glazer puts it, those sympathetic to the poor may claim,

> If there are families headed by women, it testifies to their strength. If there are more illegitimate children, it testifies to greater honesty and greater love of children. . . . If there is mistrust, it is an accurate reaction to the nature of the environment. Indeed, there is no culture of poverty at all. There is simply sensible, strong and adequate response to environment.

Something of the reaction Glazer fears is found in Frederick Holliday's comments on his paper. Holliday asserts,

> I also make the counter argument that families headed by black women show strength and not weakness. Further, I assert, black life is a sensibly conditioned response to a hostile environment. . . .

Glazer himself appears willing to recognize strengths in the culture of poverty; however, he is fearful that a "backlash" that overemphasizes the point might lead to a refusal to recognize and deal with "grave and lacerating problems." "There has been," he asserts, "a lot of loose talk about the strength of the culture of poverty. There is strength, but those who exercise it would, it is my impression, gladly exchange the test that calls it forth for a stabler and more dependable existence."

Hylan Lewis discusses the second "backlash" against Oscar Lewis' description of the so-called culture of poverty. He believes the concept has contributed to the "increasing estrangement of the poor, the black, and the youth from old line intellectuals and established men of science," and led them to question the "credibility, the relevance, the politics, and the humanity" of social scientists. The basis of the estrangement lies in the fear that stressing the persistence of the pejorative aspects of the culture of poverty lends support to those who wish to put an end to the governmental efforts to combat poverty by labeling them "obvious failures." Something of the estrangement of which Hylan Lewis speaks is found in Holliday's comments on Glazer's paper. Holliday observes that while "comments on the culture of poverty are sociological in tone, they are open to political rebuttal which the undetermined bounds of sociology should consider. . . ." He goes on to call upon blacks to "find ways to respond to arguments that are presented in the name of [social] science but ignore the political consequences."

## II. THE CULTURE OF POVERTY AS A TRUE CULTURE

### a. Lewis' Hypothesis

Lewis contends that the characteristics of the culture of poverty listed above comprise not merely a distinctive way of life, but a true *culture,* or, more accurately, a true subculture. That is, he claims that it is a pattern which, while it represents adaptation and reaction to material and social conditions, has a life of its own and is passed on from generation to generation. The perpetuation of the so-called culture of poverty is not to be explained by the continuation of the material and social conditions in which it is found. Its perpetuation is the result of socialization; it is learned by children from adults. As a culture, it has developed a degree of independence from the objective conditions in which it occurs and would persist beyond the termination of those conditions. Thus, he hypothesizes,

The culture of poverty . . . is not only an adaptation to a set of objective conditions of the larger society. Once it comes into existence it tends to perpetuate itself from generation to generation because of its effects on the children. By the time slum children are age six or seven they have usually absorbed the basic values and attitudes of their subculture and are not psychologically geared to take full advantage of changing conditions or increased opportunities which may occur in their lifetime.[8]

He goes on to claim that "the elimination of physical poverty *per se* may not be enough to eliminate the culture of poverty which is a whole way of life."[9]

### b. Social Scientific Criticisms

Two of the contributors to this volume challenge Lewis' contention that the persistence of a culture of poverty, at least in America, is the result of cultural transmission from parent to child. Both Willie and Elliot Liebow suggest that the persistence of a culture of poverty reflects the persistence of the objective conditions to which it is a response. Willie refers to continuing racial discrimination, and Liebow to the powerful political, economic and social forces that create poverty and set the circumstances for the way of life Lewis calls the "culture of poverty." Moreover, since the conditions referred to by Willie and Liebow are and have long been both contemporary and coterminous with the so-called culture of poverty, it would be difficult indeed to demonstrate that their persistence does not alone account for the persistence of a "culture of poverty."

### c. Possible Negative Consequences

Lewis' contention that the so-called culture of pov-

8 *Ibid.,* p. xlv.
9 *Ibid.,* p. lii.

erty constitutes a *true* culture—that it is a distinct way of life that would survive the elimination of the objective conditions that spawned it—was undoubtedly the most disturbing of his three hypotheses. It was feared that the claim that the poor had their own distinct culture could be used to justify ending attempts to reduce poverty by reforming the educational, occupational and political structures that create and maintain poverty. Specifically, there was concern that considering the way of life of the poor to be a *culture* could lend support to the view that it is futile to try to eliminate or limit adherence to the culture of poverty by reducing poverty. The presumed futility of efforts to end the culture of poverty would lie in the claim that, as a culture, it is passed on from generation to generation, relatively unaffected by environmental changes, and efforts to change the culture through changes in educational, political or occupational structures in the environment of the poor are apt not to work. As Lewis is quoted above, ". . . the elimination of poverty *per se* may not be enough to eliminate the culture of poverty . . . ." Holliday warns of the "ever present danger" that "if we prove that there is a culture of poverty existing today in spite of governmental efforts to raise living standards for all, some officials may question efforts to erase poverty."

In a sense, then, the stress on the inherited nature of the pejorative aspects of the culture of poverty—its passage from generation to generation regardless of changes in the environment—is, as Hylan Lewis notes, "chillingly like the idea of race." The mechanism of inheritance differs, social rather than biological; still, the core notion is that some individuals and groups are, in a meaningful sense, *inherently* different and inferior. Moreover, as Hylan Lewis goes on to observe,

> The idea of inherited poverty, as did the idea of race before

it, took on a new significance as it came to be supported by scientific trappings and the assertions of some behavioral scientists.

Opposition to attempts to eliminate poverty on grounds that they are doomed to futility can now be said to be based on scientific findings about the culture of poverty and not on bias or self-interest.

## III. THE ORIGINS OF THE CULTURE OF POVERTY

### a. Lewis' Hypothesis

Lewis is quite explicit in his claim that poverty *per se* is not solely responsible for the culture of poverty. He notes quite clearly that it is possible for a people to be poor without manifesting the culture of poverty. He cites examples of poor who do not have a culture of poverty, including primitive or preliterate peoples, lower caste Indians, and the Jews of eastern Europe. He also observes

> ... that although there is still a great deal of poverty in the United States ... there is relatively little of what I would call the culture of poverty; ... only about 20 percent of the population below the poverty line ... in the United States have characteristics which would justify classifying their way of life as that of a culture of poverty.

In sum, the culture of poverty appears only among some of the poor, but by no means all. Specifically, the poor among whom the culture of poverty tends to flourish and grow are, according to Lewis, those found in societies with the following set of conditions:

> (1) a cash economy, wage labor and production for profit; (2) a persistently high rate of unemployment and under-employment for unskilled labor; (3) low wages; (4) the failure to provide social, political and economic organization, either on a voluntary basis or by government imposition,

for the low-income population; (5) the existence of a bilateral kinship system rather than a unilateral one; and finally, (6) the existence of a set of values in the dominant class which stresses the accumulation of wealth and property, the possibility of upward mobility and thrift, and explains low economic status as the result of personal inadequacy or inferiority.[10]

The culture of poverty is most apt to be found among the poor in a stratified, highly individualized, capitalistic society. Initially, at least, the culture of poverty represents an adaptation and reaction among the poor to their marginal position within such a society and to the feelings of despair and hopelessness that develop from the realization of the improbability of achieving success as defined by the larger society. Much of the culture of poverty represents attempts by the poor to solve problems not soluble by them within existing institutions and agencies.[11]

### b. Social Scientific Criticisms

Of the contributors to this volume, only Glazer challenges Lewis' views on the origins of the so-called culture of poverty. He does so on two grounds. First, he argues that the culture of poverty does *not* appear in Hong Kong, where the conditions cited by Lewis as causes of the culture of poverty are quite prevalent. Second, the culture of poverty *does* appear in New York City, where the conditions cited by Lewis are not present. Thus, Glazer concludes, the culture of poverty need not result from the conditions cited by Lewis and may in fact result from quite different factors even in the absence of poverty *per se.*

Glazer discusses three factors, other than those cited by Lewis, as playing a role in the creation of a culture of

10 *Ibid.,* pp. xliii-xliv.
11 *Ibid.,* p. xliv.

poverty. The first is differences among the attitudes towards dependency on the part of various ethnic groups or cultures. That is, Glazer believes that certain groups or cultures have a resistance to dependency while others are more willing to accept it and thus develop a culture of poverty. Second, Glazer suggests that a culture of poverty may be fostered by the very social policies and programs that seek to eliminate poverty. He indicates that the rules of eligibility, the methods of provision of relief and the administrative practices of our welfare programs may have the unintended side effect of creating and sustaining the very dependence and poverty they officially seek to end. Finally, Glazer suggests that many of the recent changes in modern society create a climate that facilitates the growth of a culture of poverty. He cites such changes as the downgrading of thrift and foresight, the growing aversion to hard work and the erosion of the family as an institution. These changes would tend to support such characteristics of the culture of poverty as a lack of impulse control, irresponsibility and weak family ties. The existence of these three factors leads Glazer to suggest that not only is it possible, as Lewis recognizes, to have abject poverty without a culture of poverty, as among eastern European Jews, but it is possible to have a culture of poverty without abject poverty as, in Glazer's eyes, is the case among many of America's underprivileged groups.

### c. Possible Negative Consequences

The possible negative consequences of Lewis' views on the origins of the so-called culture of poverty are relatively obvious. If Lewis is wrong about the factors that originally spawn the culture of poverty, as Glazer claims, for example, then anti-poverty programs based on his views are likely, at best, to be ineffective and, at worst, harmful; and truly appropriate and effective programs based on more accurate assessments would not be designed and implemented as long as his views prevail. However, if Lewis is right that the roots of the culture of poverty in America must be traced to the character of such basic institutions as capitalism, then its elimination may not be possible short of revolution. On the other hand, if Glazer is correct that the roots of the culture of poverty in America are found not so much in capitalism as in the peculiar nature of the American welfare system, then reform and not revolution would suffice. Thus, an understanding of the nature of the culture of poverty and its roots is crucially important to the question of how best to respond to the existence of poverty within America's affluent society. It is hoped that the contents of this volume will add to the needed understanding.

# 1

## THE CULTURE OF POVERTY: THE VIEW FROM NEW YORK CITY

### NATHAN GLAZER

Oscar Lewis' most valuable contribution to the concept of the culture of poverty was to make it clear—or clearer—that there are various ways of being poor and that some are better than others. On the basis of his experiences with the poor in India, Mexico, Puerto Rico and New York, Lewis argued that the material realities of poverty in various settings—overcrowding, few capital goods, private or public, insufficient and unvaried food, difficulty of access to consumption goods, medical aid, and education—have varied consequences in varied social settings.

In India, for example, the lower castes and the untouchables lived at a level of material deprivation unmatched in the slums of Mexico City, and certainly not equaled in the slums of San Juan. The expected social consequences did not follow. Indeed, the whole

point of the culture of poverty hypothesis was that
there are no inevitable social consequences of a level of
deprivation. The lower castes in India were organized
into social units—families, kin groups, castes—that main-
tained a certain degree of solidarity, and in doing so
they could exercise, even at that deprived material level,
some degree of power to assist the members of their
group. In addition, these social forms made up part of a
whole complex of forms that gave each group its
legitimacy, its role, its modicum of power in the society,
and even, if one lived as part of the system, some degree
of respect. If one had the official place of sweeper of
the village's offal, since it was a place that had come
down by inheritance and was justified and explained in
the common religion and beliefs, it gave one a position,
even though the formal attitude toward it did involve
formal disrespect. The sweeper thus also had his dignity.
This may be excessively romantic: but there are things
in traditional India that a high-caste Hindu can and
cannot do to an untouchable.

I emphasize India because there poverty may be seen
at its worst, but the culture of poverty as Lewis has
described it is fragmentary in India; indeed, it is
questionable whether it exists there at all. On the streets
of Calcutta, where hundreds of thousands of people
sleep and live and wash and eat, a culture may be seen in
process, and it is oddly enough not the culture of
poverty. Each fragment of that humanity has important
social ties—to a village, a caste, a family—and even if
none of these ties is physically evident when one walks
down those awful streets, they are present in the mind
of each of those individuals, guiding and controlling
behavior. So work is sought, money is saved, remit-
tances are sent back to the village, children are raised
and married off.

Once again, this is perhaps idealized and romanti-
cized. There are family breakdown, prostitution, va-

grancy, abandoned children, and the like in India. But these are all viewed by those in and outside the culture of the streets as exceptional and deplorable. No one justifies illegitimacy, family abandonment, prostitution, robbery. Hard as it may be to believe, there is something middle class, from our perspective, about the way the Indian pavement dweller prepares himself for the night. The mat is spread out, the ablutions are ceremonially performed, prayers are said, the passersby are ignored.

Oscar Lewis gives two other examples of poverty that display less of the culture of poverty or lack it entirely. One is the African town, where the tribe and ethnic group still make their presence felt and organize the social life of the impoverished town-dweller, in ways not much different from the role of caste and village in India. A second example Lewis is fond of is the Jews of Eastern Europe. A third case is well recorded: the Chinese of Hong Kong, who live under conditions of crowding and deprivation far worse than found in any American big city. One estimate suggests that the amount of space an individual in a Hong Kong resettlement block has is one-tenth that available to the poor in the most crowded American cities. Families of seven and ten and fifteen live in relatively small rooms, where the only visible possessions are some clothing, a chest or two, some cooking utensils and dishes. Certainly the poor in Mexico City live under no worse physical circumstances, except that concrete blocks with water and sanitary disposal facilities are made available by the Hong Kong government. One writer points out that the level of juvenile delinquency, illegitimacy, family break-up, mental illness, and various other consequences that result from this incredible crowding are really quite moderate compared to what we might expect.[1]

[1] Robert C. Schmitt, "Implications of Density in Hong Kong," *Journal of the American Institute of Planners* (August, 1963), pp. 210-217.

In all these cases, city-dwellers manage to maintain a cultural orientation distinct from the culture of poverty. We find patriarchalism, male authority, control of children's sexual lives, fixed roles for family members that lead to some degree of confidence in how they will behave in crisis, long-range planning, both in the area of work and production and in the area of consumption, foresight in the acquisition and care of material goods.

In contrast, the culture of poverty as Oscar Lewis describes it has its own characteristics that distinguish it from poverty *per se:* the ease with which the marriage tie breaks up, or is not formed to begin with; the uncertain degree of male responsibility for children; female responsibility for children; the early induction of children into sexuality; the emphasis on present time—or limited long-range planning; mistrust between family members; mistrust of others; a feeling of helplessness and inferiority.

I have pointed out that there is poverty without the culture of poverty—Lewis gives the examples of India, East European Jews, and, more briefly, African towns. I have added Hong Kong. In addition Lewis points out that preliterate societies, despite their poverty, form no part of the "culture of poverty." Finally, the culture of poverty, he suggests, has been overcome in revolutionary Communist societies (Eastern Europe, Cuba), and in advanced welfare states. What then *is* the setting of the culture of poverty?

> In effect, we find that in primitive societies and in caste societies the culture of poverty does not develop. In socialist, fascist, and highly developed capitalist societies with a welfare state, the culture of poverty tends to decline. I suspect that the culture of poverty flourishes in, and is generic to, the early free-enterprise stage of capitalism and it is also endemic to colonialism.[2]

2 In Daniel P. Moynihan, ed., *On Understanding Poverty* (New York: Basic Books, 1969), p. 195.

In other words, for Lewis it is free enterprise capitalism in its earlier and more brutal stages that provides the setting for the culture of poverty. The conditions in which it flourishes are societies with

(1) a cash economy, wage labor, and production for profit; (2) a persistently high rate of unemployment and underemployment for unskilled labor; (3) low wages; (4) the failure to provide social, political and economic organization, either on a voluntary basis or by government imposition, for the low-income population; (5) the existence of a bilateral kinship system rather than a unilateral one; and finally, (6) the existence in the dominant class of a set of values that stresses the accumulation of wealth and property, the possibility of upward mobility, and thrift, and that explains low economic status as the result of personal inadequacy or inferiority.[3]

And yet all these features (except for number five, the bilateral kinship system, which may in any case be better seen as a characteristic of the culture of poverty rather than a cause) may be found in the exceptional areas too—Indian cities, African cities, East European Jews, Hong Kong Chinese, and we might add East European peasants.

The United States forms another problem for Lewis. It is not in the early stages of capitalism, when we might expect the culture of poverty to be epidemic. The material level at which its poor live tends to be quite high, at least in the cities, as measured simply by consumption of food, housing, clothing, and other consumer goods. Yet what Lewis has described as the culture of poverty characterizes the poor of our cities—and in particular the welfare poor—as well as it characterizes the poor of Mexico City or San Juan. Thus while Lewis has been at pains to emphasize that we can have poverty without the culture of poverty, the case of American cities raises another paradox: can we have the

3 *Ibid.,* p. 188.

33

culture of poverty without poverty? My argument is that we can, and indeed do, have it. And if we analyze the reasons for it, we must come to somewhat different conclusions as to the origins of the culture of poverty and the reasons it persists.

Do we truly have a culture of poverty without poverty in large American cities? Most of my evidence for the contention that we do is drawn from New York City.

Obviously, the term poverty may be relative as well as absolute.[4] In Oscar Lewis' usage, the emphasis has been on the absolute character of poverty, which is why he speaks of the residents of Mexico City slums, Indian cities and villages, Eastern European villages, and the preliterates everywhere, as candidates for the culture of poverty. All these groups suffer from absolute poverty. Whatever the cultural riches that may exist together with absolute poverty, absolute poverty means a primary concern with the immediate necessities of life: food, shelter, and clothing. The traditional image of the possessions of Gandhi, who took a vow of poverty, at his death is a picture of absolute poverty: some scraps of clothing, a bowl for eating, sandals, a pair of eyeglasses. Such poverty characterizes hundreds of millions in the world today. Food for the absolutely poor consists of a staple cereal, perhaps occasional vegetables. Meat, milk, and fish for the absolutely poor are rare luxuries. The culture of absolute poverty is recorded in the folklore of the very poor. "When a Jew eats chicken," an old Jewish joke runs, "one of the two is sick." Clothes are rags and shelters are shacks. The expensive public capital goods that serve even poor city-dwellers in advanced and wealthy countries—clean water supplies piped into every home, systems of sewage and garbage removal, electricity—are unknown or rare.

4 On this, see Walter Miller, "The Elimination of the American Lower Class as National Policy," in Moynihan, *op. cit.*

Having pointed all this out, we can see that there is hardly any absolute poverty in New York. Those who are ill-clothed or ill-fed—and we see many on the streets of New York—are more commonly victims of mental illness than of poverty in the absolute sense. Even if we consider the worst aspect of the life of the poor in New York—housing—we find that almost no units in the city are without hot and cold running water, fully equipped kitchens, flush toilets and baths for individual units. Very few of the poor in New York live in units in which they must double up with other families. Yet New York's housing for the poor is worse than that of other large cities. But in contrast to Mexico City, San Juan, Hong Kong, Eastern Europe and immigrants in the city itself fifty years ago, lavish and modern housing accommodations are available to the poor. If we consider food or clothing, we are even more hard put to argue that a level of absolute deprivation prevails in the city.

For a statistical picture, consider the following. In 1960 only 5 percent of white households and 10 percent of black households with incomes under $4,000 in large cities lacked "adequate" housing (that is, housing with hot and cold piped water, private kitchen, private flush toilet and bath, less than one person per room), telephone and television.[5]

Is it relevant, one may ask, to inquire into the level of absolute poverty in such a city as New York, the wealthiest in the world by some measures? I would argue that it is if we are to talk about the culture of poverty, because some of its key aspects, as presented by Lewis, must derive in large measure from absolute conditions of poverty. Thus, the terrible overcrowding

[5] Task Force on Economic Growth and Opportunity, *The Concept of Poverty*, 2, Washington, 1967, pp. 122-123, as reported in Irving H. Welfeld, "A New Framework for Federal Housing Aids," *Columbia Law Review*, LXIX (1969), 1367.

facilitates early sexual experience. The difficulty of acquiring the necessities of life encourages competition, double-dealing and mistrust in the family. The insecurity of life encourages an emphasis on the present and hedonism. All these themselves encourage the breakup of families and the abandonment of children. If, then, the culture of poverty is the result of conditions of absolute poverty, it is relevant to inquire into its extent in exploring the relationship between poverty and the culture of poverty.

Of course we know there is poverty in New York City, but it is poverty relative to a standard of living defined as necessary to a decent life by individuals, groups, and the mass media. The problem with using measures of relative poverty to explore the relationship between the culture of poverty and poverty itself is twofold. First, as we have already pointed out, it is the conditions of absolute poverty that we expect will lead—in some cases if not all—to "the culture of poverty." Thus, if as certain analysts confidently expect, families with an income of $15,000 by present standards will be considered poor by the turn of the century, we would certainly not expect them to show any features of "the culture of poverty." Second, we have another problem in using relative measures of poverty, and that is, relative to whom?

Jason Epstein some years ago asserted in the *New York Review of Books* that it took $50,000 a year to live in New York City. *New York* magazine, more recently, demonstrated how one can be poor in New York on $80,000 a year. On that basis, just about everyone in New York is poor. Dropping from this ridiculous level to define "relative" poverty, the Bureau of Labor Statistics defined in 1967 a "modest but adequate standard of living" in New York City as requiring $9,400 for a family of four. Sixty-three percent of New York's population falls below that line, and thus presumably maintained an "inadequate" standard of living. Poor families, using the Social Security Administration's poverty line of $3,500 for a family of four, include 15.3 percent of the population, which brings us closer to a reasonable definition of relative poverty.

It seems obvious that one should be able to define a meaningful measure of relative poverty in New York City, which would enable one to focus on a target population and suggest policies that may be undertaken by a modern welfare society to alleviate and overcome poverty. But the matter is not that simple. It is very hard to draw a line that differentiates the "poor" from the "not poor" and yet does not encompass within the poor a large part of the population of this most affluent society, including many who are working and in no way candidates for the "culture of poverty" and many who do not deem themselves, if we take account of their behavior, poor. The social scientists Richard A. Cloward and Frances Fox Piven have become well known for pointing to the discrepancy between those eligible for welfare and those who apply for it. Cloward and Piven helped launch a campaign to teach those eligible and not on welfare to apply—to teach them, in other words, that they were "poor," at least in the sense that they were eligible for welfare. Recently they demonstrated in an article entitled "The Poor Against Themselves" that a good part of the working population of New York City is eligible for welfare on the basis of economic criteria; that is, they earned less than a family on welfare would get and by the laws of New York State were eligible for wage supplements.[6]

To give an example, a family with three children, the oldest in college, would be eligible under welfare for $4,916. But if someone in the family worked and they

6 *Nation* (November 25, 1969).

received wage supplements, their maximum income could be $5,736. On the wage supplement (which, if there was one worker employed at the minimum wage, would be $2,616), they would pay no federal, state, or local income tax. They would also be eligible for completely free medical care. Cloward and Piven urged those in such circumstances to apply for welfare, in the form of wage supplement. They estimated that 150,000 to 300,000 working families in New York City were eligible for such supplements, and that only 12,000 applied for them. Because of ignorance, embarrassment, or because they did not consider themselves poor, this huge population, perhaps ten to twenty percent of the population of the city, did not apply for welfare.

To consider another example, David Gordon has estimated that about sixty percent of those in New York City eligible for welfare (on the basis of economic criteria) apply.[7] Once again, we find that forty percent of the eligible population do not apply for welfare.

What can we conclude? Only that the welfare payment levels in New York City are such that it is a voluntary act for many families whether they apply or not. We do not know why those who do not apply engage in this act of self-denial. Ignorance, perhaps, although the Welfare Rights Organization has done its best to enlighten them. Shame (in their own eyes or in those of others) in defining themselves as a welfare case. Cultural standards, perhaps, which define their income as adequate, even though it is not considered so by the welfare authorities. I do not know how those not on welfare and earning less than welfare would give them define their situation, but I would guess that many of them do not consider themselves desperately poor.[8]

[7] David Gordon, "Income and Welfare in New York City," *The Public Interest* (Summer 1969), p. 84.

[8] On the question of whether the poor consider themselves poor, or workers, or poor but honest, or some other category that is not simply

It would thus be a travesty to expect to find a "culture of poverty" among the so-called "working poor," who are the subject of much recent discussion. Many of them, after all, have regular union-protected jobs and children in school, some expecting to go to college. Many own their own homes, worry about inflation and taxes, discipline their children, and are concerned about the sexual revolution. If these are the poor, they do not show the characteristics of the culture of poverty—along with Lewis' examples of Indians, Jews, and preliterates.

My point is that in New York City the culture of poverty has become divorced from the conditions of poverty themselves. We have the poor who do not show the culture of poverty, as Lewis pointed out. But more significantly, we have the nonpoor—at least in terms of absolute measures of poverty—who do. One of the most striking examples of the divorce of conditions of poverty from the culture of poverty may be seen in the enormous increase in the welfare population of the city in recent years. During the past ten years in New York City, the number of the poor, by any measure, has grown at most only slightly. But the number of those on welfare has increased enormously, almost tripling.

Now the number on welfare may be taken as a crude measure of the population subject to the culture of poverty. For by far the greatest part of those on welfare are women and children who have been abandoned by husbands, male friends, and fathers. If one sees the weakness of the marital and parental ties—as I see it—as *the* key characteristic of the culture of poverty, the welfare population can be seen as a crude approximation of those subject to this culture. Admittedly there are those on welfare whose husbands have been

"poor," see Stephen J. Schensul, J. Anthony Paredes, and Peretti J. Petto, "The Twilight Zone of Poverty: A New Perspective on a Financially Depressed Area," *Human Organization*, XXVII (1968), 30-40.

killed or hurt as well as some whose husbands have joined them on welfare as complete families under the provisions of various programs that permit welfare aid to complete families with unemployed earners. But these are few. A study of a sample of families on the various family programs of the New York City Department of Welfare (Aid to Dependent Children, Temporary Aid to Dependent Children, and Home Relief) bears out my general characterization. Husbands were in residence in only one-quarter of the households, and the overwhelming majority of mothers who were without husbands were separated (forty percent of the sample) or unmarried (twenty percent of the sample). Divorce was responsible for a mother without a husband in five percent of the families; widowhood in only five percent.[9] Thus, if welfare aid is a measure, as it seems to be, of abandonment and illegitimacy, this has increased enormously in recent years despite the fact that we find no increase in the number of the poor.

This is not a new observation. Daniel P. Moynihan pointed out in his famous report on the Negro family that ADC cases no longer moved together with unemployment figures, but rose independently of them. Other measures also support the general argument that poverty has become divorced from the culture of poverty—for example, the steady increase in the number of families headed by women in Northern cities, particularly among blacks, and the steady if slower increase in illegitimacy, which characteristically means the fiscal abandonment of the child to state care.[10]

But if all this is so, what are we to make of it?

[9] Lawrence Podell, "Families on Welfare in New York City," Center for the Study of Urban Problems, Bernard M. Baruch College, The City University of New York (1968), p. 1.

[10] Black female-headed families in metropolitan areas of 1,000,000 or more increased 83 percent between 1960 and 1968; white, 16 percent. See "Trends in Social and Economic Conditions in Metropolitan Areas," U.S. Bureau of the Census, Current Population Reports, February 7, 1969.

Certainly Oscar Lewis' general characterization of the causes of the culture of poverty will not hold. To Lewis, it is the conditions of early and rampant capitalism that explain the culture of poverty—wages close to the survival line, the reserve army of the unemployed, the grim necessity to work at any menial or casual labor to exist, the absence of organization among the poor. And yet, those who live in and study Hong Kong view it as the sole survivor of a Victorian level of pure laissez-faire capitalism in the world. There is almost no social legislation, no free education, no requirement that children go to school, no child labor laws, no minimum wages. If one wants to find the conditions that Oscar Lewis feels lead to capitalism, go to Hong Kong. It is not only an example of the unmoderatedly fierce early stage of capitalism, but it remains one of the few existing examples in the world of an unmoderated, classic colonialism—the other feature that by Lewis' account leads to the culture of poverty. For in Hong Kong, the overwhelming majority of the population has no political rights—it does not vote—and in any case all power is held by the crown. We might extend these observations. India was and is the seat of early capitalism, somewhat stifled by efforts at central controls, social legislation, and central planning. It was the classic case of colonialism. Yet the culture of poverty is found there only in moderation.

On the other hand, in New York City we find the culture of poverty proceeding apace with the rapid development of the welfare state—higher levels of welfare, broader social insurance coverage, reduced unemployment, growing means of state assistance in seeking employment and preparing oneself for employment, and even (and this is hardly a characteristic of all welfare states, but one in which the United States has pioneered) growing organization among the welfare poor to demand higher benefits and greater power.

41

Certainly this phenomenon of the increase of the culture of poverty along with the decline of poverty deserves research—research that relatively few social scientists have carried out. I would list as two notable exceptions Elliot Liebow and Walter B. Miller. It will be of no help in illuminating this paradox to insist rather blindly and ahistorically that there is no paradox. There are two broad examples of the way this is done by contemporary researchers and analysts. On the one hand, there are those who insist that poverty in the United States is rampant and not declining. This is done not only by political leaders. One can also find examples of this insistence on the denial of the best facts and information we have among the social scientists. Those who dismiss the paradox by asserting that the number of the poor remains as large as it has always been and their conditions as deplorable have an obligation to analyze the Census and Bureau of Labor statistics and demonstrate that these figures are misleading or wrong. Such an approach would contribute more than simple assertions, which may testify to their sympathy and morality but not to their ability as social scientists.[11]

There is a second and to my mind sadder means of dismissing the paradox: to deny that what we have is a culture of poverty in the pejorative sense of that term at all. If there are families headed by women, it testifies to their strength. If there are more illegitimate children, it testifies to greater honesty and greater love of children. If there is a greater rate of abandonment, it is owing only to the agony of being unable to provide adequate support. If there is mistrust, it is an accurate reaction to the nature of the environment. Indeed, there is no culture of poverty at all. There is simply sensible, strong, and adequate response to environment. Here too we find more assertion of the case than demonstration.

[11] On this general point, see Stephen Thernstrom's excellent article, "Poverty in Historical Perspective," in Moynihan, *op. cit.*

We find little research to demonstrate that within this culture there is greater love of children, more accurate perceptions of the world, greater honesty, and all the rest.

I say this is a sad way of dismissing the paradox because to my mind it refuses to recognize grave and lacerating problems. Indeed, this kind of denial often shows a class blindness. The well-to-do hedonist and bohemian can, to be sure, through choice and with fewer long-range consequences lead a life of casual alliances. But he leaves fewer children behind to be raised by abandoned and despairing and angry women; or if he does, he can generally provide monetary support for them. There has been a lot of loose talk about the strength of the culture of poverty. There is strength, but those who exercise it would, it is my impression, gladly exchange the test that calls it forth for a stabler and more dependable existence.

But if we cannot deny the paradox, what can we make of it? Here I become more speculative. I return to Lewis' distinction between the cultures that, in poverty, develop a culture of poverty, and those that seem capable of maintaining, simply, a culture. One cannot help being impressed by the variations with which certain groups resort to welfare. Thus, in New York City, two-fifths of the Puerto Rican population is on welfare, and, somewhat further behind, one-third of the black. A study of a sample of the population of the West Side of New York, which includes a substantial number of Cubans and Haitians and other Caribbean and Latin American groups, shows a strikingly low proportion of welfare cases among them, only 10 percent, compared to 21 percent of those raised in New York City, 44 percent of those raised in Puerto Rico, 26 percent of those raised in the southern United States, 10 percent of those raised in the northeastern United States, and only 8 percent of those raised elsewhere, presumably European and Asian immigrants. What is the cause of these differences? Gross observation suggests that it cannot be explained simply by differences in literacy, occupation, skill, and the like, though these certainly play a role. It does seem that certain cultures resist dependency, as others accept it. It would be important to understand these phenomena better, for we are saying very little by merely asserting that one culture "resists" dependency and another "accepts" it.

If we understood these differences better, could we do much about them? After all, we are hardly likely to become social engineers of culture. Nevertheless, I believe this could be a fruitful line of investigation. Just as the investigations into ethnic and racial differences in educational achievement begin to give us certain glimmers of lines of action that might perhaps improve achievement, so research into culture differences in behavior in connection with dependency could give us some insight into policy measures that might be successful there. Of course it is hardly likely that we could agree on policy measures if we fail to agree that the culture of poverty demands some intervention or amelioration, or that dependence is worse than independence. And unfortunately many do not agree on these points.

A second highly hypothetical line of investigation is suggested to me by the odd fact that the culture of poverty and dependency seems to expand—at least in this country—along with the policy measures designed to deal with it. Thus our steady tinkering with welfare has been accompanied by a steady increase in the welfare population. Even the proposals of President Nixon, the most radical since the adoption of federal support for public assistance in 1937, begin with another huge increase in the population to be aided. Other aspects of these revolutionary changes are designed to transform the stigma of welfare into the positively valued new program of family assistance, but one must cross one's fingers as to whether such a radical change in identity can be accomplished easily, or at all. I am impressed by the observation of Tocqueville, 135 years ago, in his "Memoir on Pauperism," that the most prosperous nation in Europe (England) had a much higher rate of dependency than the poorest states (Spain and Portugal), and that the most prosperous parts of France had much higher rates of dependency than the least prosperous. Tocqueville did not resort to any differences in culture in explaining this, but insisted that dependency would have to increase with prosperity and enlightenment. Education would lead to new tastes and new desires, the expansion of transportation and communication would permit new invidious comparisons, inevitably prosperity would mean dependency.

> We should not delude ourselves [he wrote] .... As long as the present movement of civilization continues, the standard of living of the greatest number will rise: the society will become more perfected, better informed; existence will be easier, milder, more embellished, and longer. But at the same time we must look forward to an increase of those who will need to resort to the support of all their fellow men to obtain a small part of these benefits. It will be possible to moderate this double movement; special national circumstances will precipitate or suspend its course; but no one can stop it.[12]

Tocqueville went on to analyze, correctly I think, the inevitable effects of public charity, which could only be degrading. He did not envisage that it could be turned into a right, so that it could be stripped of its degrading character. This is a hope we now cling to. We speak of redefining dependencies into something ennobling. We have not sufficiently analyzed how complex such an operation must be. Once again to quote Tocqueville:

[12] Quoted in Seymour Drescher, *Tocqueville and Beaumont on Social Reform* (New York: Harper, 1968), p. 11.

There is something great and virile in the idea of right
which removes from any bequest its suppliant character,
and places the one who claims it on the same level as the
one who grants it. But the right of the poor to obtain
society's help is unique in that instead of elevating the heart
of the man who exercises it, it lowers him. . . . From the
moment that an indigent is inscribed on the poor list of his
parish he can certainly demand relief, but what is the
achievement of this right if not a notarized manifestation of
misery, of weakness, of misconduct on the part of its
recipient? Ordinary rights are conferred on men by reason
of some personal advantage acquired by them over their
fellow men. This other kind is accorded by reason of a
recognized inferiority. The first is a clear statement of
superiority; the second publicizes inferiority and legalizes
it. The more extensive and secure ordinary rights are, the
more honor they confer; the more permanent and extended
the right to relief is, the more it degrades.

We can suggest then two hypotheses—that cultures
show a variable resistance to features of the culture of
poverty and to the dependency that is its consequence
in advanced welfare states; and that social policy itself
must increase the number of those who become dependent, not only by simply providing for relief, but by
mechanisms of eligibility, provision, and administration
that have various side effects leading to features of the
culture of poverty and dependency. Now it is possible
that in certain ways the culture of modern society itself,
of welfare state society, takes on features that encourage the culture of poverty. Here I cannot do better
than quote from Thernstrom:

A . . . change which demands attention is the steady erosion
of the subcultures which defined the expectations of
working men in the past. There were once working-class-en-
claves—often, but not necessarily—with ethnic boundaries—
within which the mobility values of the society were
redefined in more attainable terms. The workingmen of
nineteenth-century America toiled with remarkable dedica-

tion to accumulate the funds to pay for tiny cottages of their own and were amazingly successful at it. . . . But everything about contemporary American society conspires to make . . . having lower aspirations than others more difficult. . . . Many of the poor today expect more and put up with less from others in order to get it, precisely because the enclaves of old have been levelled, with all the docility and deference which they fostered. Of course one can always say this represents a weakening of the moral fibre of the common man, . . . but the point is that this weakening of the moral fibre, if you wish to call it that, is no accident; it is not a mere passing whim, but the result of some large and irreversible changes in society.

It is obvious that this line of argument applies with special force to the Negro. His objective grievances are real enough, . . . but they are by no means new. . . .[13]

Thernstrom then points to the startling changes in the levels of demand by the dependent, for example, the demands of the Welfare Rights organizations, and points out they were unimaginable in the past but must continue to rise in the future. And he concludes: "The American Negro has never lived in the thrift-oriented subculture of the classic European immigrant. . . . This is no longer the nineteenth century and there is no way of isolating the ghetto from the mass media and inundating it with McGuffey's readers. . . ."[14]

In effect, changes in modern society itself—the downgrading of thrift, foresight, hard work, family responsibility—combine with certain features of existing subcultures, and give them greater legitimacy and greater general acceptance, and those who carry its features therefore show a new self-confidence in asserting that their ways, too, have virtue—perhaps exceptional virtue—and demand support. ·

If then, as Tocqueville wrote, public charity grows

[13] *Op. cit.,* pp. 180f.
[14] *Ibid.*

with the increase of prosperity, of education, of knowledge, all of which raise desires and expectations; if it has degrading consequences, despite its origin in the virtuous desire to alleviate distress, what are our alternatives? To let people starve is impossible; even to allow them to exist on, or fall to a standard of living that all our laws and regulations condemn and even ban, is quite out of the question. Our most useful alternatives are to try to expand the measures that might prevent a resort to public charity as a right. If more of those who might fall subject to the culture of poverty could be induced to remain on the farms and in the small towns through proper rewards; if more could be assisted to higher paying jobs, which themselves carried various insurances, that is, "rights"—health, unemployment, sick leaves, and the like; if more of the costs of raising a family could be shifted to funds that could indeed be granted as of right, rather than on the basis of special appeal, a means test, and a special determination; then perhaps the inevitably increasing demand of the poor—and the nonpoor too—to a higher measure of public insurance and support could be met in ways that were not degrading. In short, our task is to translate demeaning charity into rights. But it is not to be done as simply as many now think, by fiat and renaming. It can only be done by subtle and close attention to what most people understand by right and what most people understand as unworthy privilege. It will involve hard and close work to expand the realm of right, and narrow as much as we can the domain defined as charity.

# COMMENTS ON "THE CULTURE OF POVERTY: THE VIEW FROM NEW YORK CITY"

## FREDERICK D. HOLLIDAY

Nathan Glazer cites a paradox derived from Oscar Lewis' ideas on the culture of poverty: the expected social consequences of poverty in some societies are not readily evident. As a case in point, the street people of India, in great measure, do not exhibit the culture of poverty as Lewis describes it.

Some characteristics of the culture of poverty Glazer attributes to Lewis are: the incidence of marriage breakups; marriages not legally formed; lack of male responsibility for children; early induction of children into sexual activity; limited long-range planning; mistrust between family members and others; and feelings of helplessness and inferiority.

In the United States, particularly among poor blacks, the culture of poverty continues to develop though actual poverty conditions are decreasing.[1] Female-headed households and illegitimacy continue to rise, although welfare grants are liberalized and family income increases.[2] Further, self-concept among blacks is lower than among similar groups of whites.[3]

Glazer asks whether a culture of poverty can exist without conditions of poverty. He answers, yes, and

[1] U. S. Department of Commerce, *Population Characteristics,* series P-20, No. 189 (Washington: Government Printing Office, August 18, 1969).

[2] U. S. Department of Commerce, *Recent Trends in Social and Economic Conditions of Negroes in the United States,* series P-23, No. 26 (Washington: Government Printing Office, July 1968),

[3] U. S. Department of Health, Education, and Welfare, *Equality of Educational Opportunity* (Washington: Government Printing Office, 1966).

proposes "the weakness of the marital and parental tie as the key characteristic of the culture of poverty." Continuing, Glazer states that Lewis' idea that a culture of poverty flourishes in the early developing stages of free enterprise capitalism and that it is endemic to colonialism would be difficult to prove in the United States, for this country is beyond that stage.

This assumption by Glazer is not true, as is evident when one considers the condition of blacks in this country. The very existence among whites of a set of values that stresses the accumulation of wealth and property and the promise of upward mobility to those who persevere, but denies equal access to opportunities for black people is a description of colonialism.

The marks of colonialism, as Fanon states them, are military occupation, economic exploitation, and the destruction of indigenous culture.[4] The worldwide results, as seen by the ruling caste, are: self-hatred, feelings of inferiority, and deviation from so-called normal family and sex roles. Colonialism does not have to exist outside of a particular homeland. It can and does exist wherever one or more segments of the population differ from other segments by reason of race, religion, or economic condition. Negroes, according to Kroeber, although interlocked in American society are not really part of it. Thus, it is unscientific to represent the mores of whites as the normal, and those of blacks as abnormal.

The lack of male authority, the inability to control a child's early entrance into sex life, and the failure to plan and care for material goods cannot be accepted as the stigmata of the culture of poverty. Nor can the converse be accepted as the marks of the culture of the

[4] On this, see Frantz Fanon, *The Wretched of the Earth* (New York: Grove, 1968); *Black Skin—White Masks* (New York: Grove, 1967); *A Dying Colonialism* (New York: Grove, 1965); *Toward the African Revolution* (New York: Grove, 1967).

privileged. Blacks have the right to challenge the validity of the definition of a culture of poverty as discussed by Glazer. His assumptions suffer from a kind of verbal reasoning that cannot be scientifically proved.

What is needed is a second look at ways that hard data can be put to use by social scientists. For example, one of Glazer's indicators of the culture of poverty is the instability of the family. The Negro family, according to the Census Bureau, is increasingly headed by women. During the period 1967-1969, the percentage changed from 25 to 29 percent.[5] Additionally, one birth in four among Negroes is without benefit of clergy. But, fully one-third of all first-born among those married were conceived before the ceremony. This study included blacks and whites.

Rather than conclude at this time that the culture of poverty is accelerating though poverty is declining, additional questions should be raised, which may cause sociologists to take a second look at the hard data before interpreting them in such a way that political overtones may militate against blacks. One example is the data which show that more Negro families are headed by women, and that so-called illegitimacy is seven times the rate for whites. This is now open to question. It is premature to draw the conclusion that economic indicators are rising while the culture of poverty is increasing, unless the causes of the data used are examined further. For instance, some additional questions to explore are: whether Myrdal is correct in his assertion that poor blacks' abhorrence of oral-genital contact is a factor in higher rates of illegitimacy;[6] whether the difference between black and white illegitimacy rates is the white abortion rate; whether the

[5] U. S. Department of Commerce, *Population Characteristics,* series P-20, No. 189.

[6] Gunnar Myrdal, *An American Dilemma* (New York: Harper, 1944), Vol. 1.

absence of one parent from the home prevents control of a child's entry into sexual activity; whether whites make use of contraceptive chemicals and devices because of more favored economic conditions; and whether the African-extended family as part of black American culture is operative.

Because there are so many questions that have not been raised and carefully examined, I take what Dr. Glazer calls the "sadder means" of dismissing the paradox that while poverty is diminishing the culture of poverty is increasing in the United States. I also make the counter argument that families headed by black women show strength and not weakness. Further, I assert, black life is a sensibly conditioned response to a hostile environment that has permitted the race to survive. The life styles of blacks have been developed in isolation; black differences are normal and not abnormal, and should not be compared to whites in the "superior" caste.[7]

While Dr. Glazer's comments on the culture of poverty are sociological in tone, they are open to political rebuttal, which the undetermined bounds of sociology should consider and, hopefully, incorporate at some future time. Blacks must find ways to respond to arguments that are presented in the name of science but ignore the political consequences. Blacks must find ways to raise questions and set their own social agenda and not merely continue to respond to questions raised by others.

There is always danger in the kind of thing we are doing today. If we prove that a culture of poverty exists today in spite of governmental efforts to raise living standards for all, some officials may question efforts to erase poverty. Or, conversely, suppose additional pov-

[7] Robert Redfield, *The Primitive World and Its Transformation* (Ithaca: Cornell University Press, 1953).

erty might be created to force blacks and other poor to abandon a culture of poverty that is said to include having babies, wasting money, and living for the moment. Politically, sentiments toward blacks can take the form held in bygone days. The liberality of sociologists now being heard can be stifled. The academic teasing we engage in today may be interpreted by those politicians in power in such a way as to be used against people we are intending to help. This is the danger of not dissecting in all possible ways every assumption that has social consequences. The culture of poverty, because it has political as well as social consequences, must be set aside as a valid means of explaining our society. People, in this case black, must share in what we consider as legitimate socio-political-economic aspirations and modes of behavior.

# 2

## FAMILY STRUCTURE, POVERTY AND RACE

### CHARLES V. WILLIE

To begin this discussion on family structure, poverty and race, let us consider a few black facts of life. These facts come primarily from the Bureau of the Census and the Bureau of Labor Statistics. Unless stated otherwise, data were obtained from Current Population Surveys in 1967 and 1968.[1]

In 1968, the Negro population was estimated at 22 million, or 11 percent of the total United States population.

Negro people largely are city dwellers.

The prevailing pattern of family life among Negro people is the conjugal unit or the nuclear household consisting of husband, wife, and children. Both spouses are present in seventy percent of all Negro families.

[1] U. S. Department of Commerce, *Recent Trends in Social and Economic Conditions of Negroes in the United States;* Bureau of the Census, "Negro Population: March 1967," *Current Population Reports* (Washington: Government Printing Office, 1968).

55

Most Negro households are supported by the work of a man. More than ninety percent of adult black men in the labor force are employed.

Nearly one-third of the black families have incomes less than $3,000 a year and only about half of these poor families receive public welfare. Black families are forced to make do with a median income that is forty percent lower than the median for whites.

These facts indicate that the Negro family is still around, that the Negro family has not broken down. These facts also point toward a prevailing pattern of family stability among black people, a family that has persevered in spite of limited resources. As stated by psychiatrist Robert Coles, "there's sinew in the Negro family."[2]

The miracle of the Negro family is that it has survived and grown stronger over the years. Gunnar Myrdal, relying heavily on the research and interpretations of the late E. Franklin Frazier of Howard University, wrote in his monumental study, *The American Dilemma,* that "most slave owners . . . did not care about the marital state of their slaves. . . ." Indeed, "the internal slave trade broke up many slave families. . . ."[3] These facts were confirmed by Frederick Douglass, who was born in slavery in 1817 and who later became an advisor to President Abraham Lincoln.

Historian Rayford Logan of Howard University calls *The Life and Times of Frederick Douglass,* the autobiography that Douglass completed in 1892, "a classic in American Literature."[4] Frederick Douglass had this to say about his family life in slavery:

[2] Robert Coles, "There's Sinew in the Negro Family," background paper for White House Conference on Civil Rights, November, 1965. Reprinted from the *Washington Post,* October 10, 1965

[3] Gunnar Myrdal, *An American Dilemma* (New York: Harper and Brothers, 1944), p. 931.

[4] In the Introduction to the reprinted edition of *The Life and Times of Frederick Douglass* (New York: Macmillan, 1962), p. 15.

The reader must not expect me to say much of my family. . . . My first experience of life, as I now remember it . . . began in the family of my grandmother and grandfather. . . . The practice of separating mothers from their children and hiring them out at distances too great to admit of their meeting, save at long intervals, was a marked feature of the cruelty and barbarity of the slave system. . . . It had no interest in recognizing or preserving any of the ties that bind families together or to their homes.

My grandmother's five daughters [one of whom was my mother] were hired out in this way, and my only recollections of my own mother are of a few hasty visits made in the night on foot, after the daily tasks were over, and when she was under the necessity of returning in time to respond to the . . . call to the field in the early morning. . . .

Of my father I know nothing. Slavery had no recognition of fathers. . . .

Old master . . . only allowed the little children to live with grandmother for a limited time; . . . as soon as they were big enough they were promptly taken away. . . . The time came when I must go. . . . I was seven years old.[5]

Frederick Douglass was an ingenious man. By the time he was 21 he had escaped from slavery. In disguise, he traveled from Maryland to New York and immediately sent for his fiancée, Anna Murray, a free woman, to come north to marry him. Frederick and Anna lived together as man and wife 44 years until Mrs. Douglass died in 1882.[6]

The above excerpts from *The Life and Times of Frederick Douglass* give a historical perspective to our considerations about the Negro family. The reflections of Douglass tell us two things: first, there was little opportunity for experiencing family life among black

[5] Douglass, *op. cit.*, pp. 27-33.

[6] *Ibid.*, pp. 204-205; see also p. 20 of Logan's Introduction.

slaves; second, former slaves were capable of forming enduring family unions. The first fact is usually remembered; the second fact is frequently forgotten.

Some social scientists have attempted to explain the higher proportion of broken families among black people than among white people as a direct outgrowth of the slavery experience. For example, Andrew Billingsley said

> The slave system had a crippling effect on the establishment, maintenance, and growth of normal patterns of family life among Negro people. . . . This crippled the development not only of individual slaves, but of families, and hence of the whole society of Negro people. . . . The consequences these conditions wrought for Negroes under the slave system were direct and insidious. The consequences for succeeding and even modern generations of Negroes are, perhaps, less direct, but no less insidious.[7]

Daniel Patrick Moynihan attempts to specify the consequences. "In essence," he said, "the Negro community has been forced into a matriarchal structure which, because it is so out of line with the rest of American society, seriously retards the progress of the group as a whole." Moynihan called this alleged matriarchal structure and its limitations the "fearful price" that the Negro American community has paid "for the incredible mistreatment to which it has been subjected over the past three centuries."[8]

The facts do not jibe with these assertions. The Negro family is *not* basically a matriarchal system. More than ninety percent of the adult black men in the labor force are working to support their households. Moreover, approximately seventy percent of the black families are two-parent families; and sixty percent of all black

[7] Andrew Billingsley, *Black Families in White America* (Englewood Cliffs, N. J.: Prentice-Hall, 1968), pp. 68f.

[8] United States Department of Labor, *The Negro Family* (Washington: Government Printing Office), p. 29.

children grow up in households in which a mother and father are present. The relationship between black and white spouses tends toward equality. The hypothesis that the slavery heritage of black people has contributed to a high rate of contemporary family instability and to a matriarchal system fails to recognize that among the intact families, which is the prevailing pattern, many members have parents, grandparents or great-grand-parents who were born in slavery and that the slavery heritage for these two-parent households has not contributed to their undoing.

Indeed the history of the Negro family must be viewed as a miraculous movement from *nothing* to *something.* In spite of the severe handicap imposed by slavery, and in spite of the disadvantaged circumstances and limited economic opportunities that black people have experienced and continue to experience in America, the Negro family as a cultural institution has been able to move during a single century of partial freedom to within 18 to 19 percentage points of the rate of two-parent household stability among white families. In 1967 seventy-one percent of all Negro families in the United States were husband-wife units, compared with eighty-nine percent of all white families.[9] In family stability (defined as a two-parent household) the black family has demonstrated an amazing pace of catching up. In one century, black people have developed a two-parent household stability among white families. In attempting to develop for more than three centuries. The efforts of the black population in this respect have been heroic. It is probable that much of the family instability among some blacks is more a function of contemporary economic circumstances and racial discrimination than of historical circumstances such as the slavery tradition.

[9] Bureau of the Census, "Negro Population," p. 3.

It is known that an indirect association exists between family income and family instability: as the family income decreases the proportion of families headed by one parent increases. This holds true for black and white families alike. This relationship is more complex than a simple linear relationship, however. In households with an income of more than $10,000 a year, there is no measurable difference in the proportion of one-parent families by race: five percent of the white families in this higher income category are headed by females, compared to six percent of the higher income black families. But among extremely poor families, with incomes under $2,000 a year, the proportion of black families headed by females (61 percent) is almost twice as great as the female-based poor white households (36 percent).[10] Why the proportions of one-parent families among white and black affluent households are similar while the proportions differ greatly among black and white poor households is a problem worthy of further investigation.

Juvenile delinquency, which has been looked upon by some social scientists as a behavioral consequence of broken families, shows a relationship to family structure and economic status that is similar for black and white racial areas where poor broken families live, but dissimilar for black and white racial areas where affluent intact families live.

My Washington, D.C., census-tract ecological studies based on juvenile delinquency court data gathered between 1959 and 1962 revealed delinquency rates of 42 and 44 per 1,000 court-referred youth in the most disadvantaged and disorganized areas, but in the affluent areas characterized by few broken families there were significantly different rates by race. The rate of 20 in

[10] U. S. Census Bureau, *Trends in Social and Economic Conditions in Metropolitan Areas,* series P-23, No. 27 (Washington: Government Printing Office, 1969).

the black area was almost twice as great as the rate of 11 in the white area.[11] Why under the most disadvantaged economic and family circumstances delinquency rates are similar for black and white populations but are different for racial groups under favorable economic and family conditions also must be further examined. These discrepancies could be a function of the analytical categories used and the cutting points imposed upon the distributions, or they could be a function of sociological circumstances.

Obviously the association between race, family status, and economic status is complex. I have not suggested a solution to these highlighted problems. I have called attention to them, however, in the hope that investigators will be alerted to the dangers of drawing premature and simplistic conclusions about the association between race, family status, and poverty, based on inadequate investigation and analysis.

In spite of the complexity of the problem, I think it is possible to develop some testable hypotheses about this theme. I attempted to develop such a few years ago in an article entitled "Intergenerational Poverty." In that article, I set forth the following argument:

> Because there are twice as many poor [black] people as there are poor whites, and because racial discrimination has been identified as a key cause which keeps Negroes at the bottom (an experience which they do not share with poor whites), it could very well be that different hypotheses are needed for explaining the continuation of poverty in the two racial populations.
>
> . . . . .
>
> Personal and family connected circumstances are likely to be more powerful explanations of poverty among whites than among [blacks].

[11] Charles V. Willie, "The Relative Contribution of Family Status and Economic Status to Juvenile Delinquency," *Social Problems*, XIV (Winter 1967), 331f.

Institutional arrangements and patterns of social organization are likely to be more powerful explanations of poverty
among blacks than among whites.[12]

The hypotheses proposed as an explanation of poverty among whites are often set forth as an explanation
of poverty among blacks. I have tried to explain why
these new and different hypotheses might be of value in
the study of poverty by race:

Institutional changes [particularly the expanding economy]
during the past three or four decades have resulted in a
substantial reduction in the proportion of whites who are
poor. External changes in social organization have upgraded
87 percent of the white population beyond the poverty
level. The 13 percent who remain poor probably have
problems which are more personal and less susceptible to
mass amelioration through institutional manipulations.
These whites may be the individuals with insufficient
motivation, low aspiration, and a fatalistic orientation
unreached thus far by changes in the institutional systems
of society which create new opportunities. The proportion
of poor Negroes, however, remains at a high level and may
still be amenable to ameliorative mass efforts. Apparently,
the kinds of institutional changes needed to upgrade the
Negro population are somewhat different from those
required to upgrade the white population [today]. In
addition to deliberate institutional changes which may
increase opportunities in an expanding economy, Negroes
require deliberate institutional changes which will prevent
racial discrimination. Until these are put into effect, we
cannot know how large the residual proportion of [black]
poor people might be who need such individualized
attention as the 13 percent of poor whites may now
require. . . .
. . . . .

Changes in institutional arrangements have been largely
responsible for preventing poverty among whites, and there
is reason to believe that such changes will aid in the

12 Charles V. Willie, "Intergenerational Poverty," *Poverty and Human
Resources Abstracts,* IV (February 1969), 12f.

prevention of poverty among [blacks] if the benefits of these changes are made available to all. . . .

Because whites, in general, have had [unobstructed] access to the opportunities produced by institutional change, the residual number of poor people in this racial category might well be a function of personal and family-connected deficiencies. It is not concluded that poverty among whites cannot be further reduced by more changes in the institutional systems of society. Rather, it is suggested that new manipulations of social institutions will probably net a smaller rate of change in the proportion of poor whites, since most whites who could benefit from these major institutional changes have already taken advantage of them.[13]

For reasons stated above, I conclude that the Moynihan plan to deal with poverty by stabilizing the family may project a solution more appropriate for poor whites upon poor blacks. The institutional changes that have rescued nearly nine out of every ten whites from poverty have not run their full course for blacks. Hence all forms of racial discrimination must be prohibited, so that the opportunities of an expanding economy may be made available to blacks. Then and only then can we determine if their family instability rather than their economic insecurity is the chief cause of their poverty.

My Washington, D. C., studies of juvenile delinquency form part of the basis for the hypothesis developed about poverty among black people. I discovered that reducing family instability would probably contribute to a greater reduction in delinquency among whites than among blacks, and that increasing economic opportunities would very likely contribute to a greater reduction in delinquency among blacks than among whites. While a good deal of family instability existed in the Negro community in Washington, D.C. (although the one-

[13] *Ibid.*

parent family there, too, was an experience of a minority of the black population), economic insecurity was overwhelming. Based on the data and analysis of my Washington study of juvenile delinquency, it appeared that one would not be successful in getting at the family instability factor without first dealing with economic insecurity. Thus a serial pattern of attack seemed to be required.

Since economic insecurity has been dealt with among whites so that only about one out of every ten remains in poverty, family instability is the outstanding problem for whites. But among blacks one out of every three continued in poverty. Until the number of black poor is reduced to a proportion similar to that now existing for the white poor, the society may be unable to deal with family instability among blacks.[14]

Meanwhile, I would suggest another approach while waiting for the data to come in to test these new hypotheses. Rather than developing a national master plan to overhaul the Negro family, I would suggest that the nation begin an intensive study of its strengths. Let us return to some of Robert Coles' observations and his findings about children who integrated southern schools. He said, "I was constantly surprised at the endurance shown by children we would call poor or . . . culturally disadvantaged. . . . What enabled such children from such families to survive emotional and educational ordeals that many white middle-class boys and girls would find impossible?"[15]

What is significant about the Negro family in America is that it has survived. Courage, endurance and ingenuity are the cultivated characteristics of Negro families in America that have contributed to their survival. By learning how the Negro family has strengthened itself

[14] Charles V. Willie, "The Relative Contribution of Family Status and Economic Status to Juvenile Delinquency."

[15] Robert Coles, *Children of Crisis* (New York: Dell, 1967).

and transcended overwhelming obstacles, we in America might learn how to strengthen the families of this nation and even the family of man.

I conclude this discussion by returning to the words and wisdom of Frederick Douglass. Reflecting upon his experiences as a slave, Douglass said, "A man's troubles are always half disposed of when he finds endurance the only alternative."[16] Such a statement is similar to one expressed by Martin Luther King, Jr., in the 1960's. Reflecting upon the civil rights struggle, King said, "if we will dare to meet [this challenge] honestly, historians in the future years will have to say there lived a great people . . . a black people . . . who bore their burdens of oppression in the heat of many days and who, through tenacity and creative commitment, injected new meaning into the veins of American life."[17] This then is the black heritage—endurance and transcendence—which in part helped the black population come to the level of family stability that it has now achieved. Thus, the task for sociologists is not to discover ways of overhauling the black family so that it may be fashioned in the image of whites. More important is the task of understanding the unique strengths in the Negro family in America that have enabled it to accomplish in one century a kind of stability similar to the stability that the white family in America has required almost three centuries to develop.

[16] Douglass, *op. cit.*, p. 39.

[17] Martin Luther King, Jr., *Where Do We Go From Here?* (Boston: Beacon Press, 1967).

# COMMENTS ON "FAMILY STRUCTURE, POVERTY AND RACE"

## HERBERT APTHEKER

Professor Willie has presented a paper offering great stimulation and a much-needed corrective in the literature on his subject.

We would suggest that in addition to Douglass' autobiography it would be germane, especially since we now have William Styron's Confessions, to note the family structure experienced by Nat Turner, the slave insurrectionist. Here one has not a slave in a border environment, as in the case of Douglass, but one living in southern, tidewater Virginia. Turner tells us that he remembered and was influenced by both his father and his mother and also his grandmother. He reports that it was his parents who taught him to read and write—extraordinary since learning to read was illegal for slaves and teaching a slave a serious crime. Turner was married, too—not in terms of a contract, of course, since this was forbidden to slaves—and his wife bore him two children. After his rebellion had failed and he was a fugitive, the contemporary Virginia press reported that his wife was severely lashed in a vain effort to gain information as to his whereabouts; after his execution the children and wife were sold out of Virginia.

The differences in family experiences between Douglass and Turner lead one to note that there were great differences during the time of slavery—and since, of course—in such experiences among black people in general. The differences were and are based upon class, location, and the like. Thus, in 1860 there were half a million free blacks, and their family structures and experiences obviously differed from those of the slaves; again, differences were great between those free blacks living in the South (about 250,000) and those in the North. Differences within regions were sharp, too: the structure of life among free blacks in New Orleans was quite different from that in Charleston and the differences between structures in Philadelphia and in Cincinnati were hardly less marked.

Significant was the fact that family status was part of the very definition of freedom; the effort to deny such status to the enslaved was a mark of their condition. There is no doubt that the effort had large measures of success but never total. Furthermore, the effort to destroy family evoked among the intended victims an effort to preserve family; it also produced among the black people an intense feeling of family and a yearning for solidarity. In this connection one must note the fairly widespread practice among pre-Civil War black people of purchasing freedom: buying one's own freedom and buying the freedom of one's loved ones. Here one had quite literally the creation, through much sweat and frugality, of a family reality. When manumission was forbidden late in slavery and purchase of one's freedom became illegal, there were not a few cases of free blacks buying a wife or a mother or a husband or a father and then continuing to "own" the purchased one for purposes of census returns; in fact, again, a family had been quite literally forged after very great effort.

Note should also be taken of the phenomenon, which reached mass proportions after the emancipation, of black people hunting for relatives (and advertising for them in the Negro press that proliferated). This continued from the 1860's until well into the 1900's and involved scores of thousands of people. It again is a unique attribute of the family history of black people in the United States. Very little has been published about this post-Civil War phenomenon, but even a cursory examination of the sources will persuade anyone that the paucity of study does not reflect insignificance of the subject.

As to the two specific problems raised in Professor Willie's paper, we suggest the following: first, all Negro women worked in slavery and the overwhelming majority have worked since; this may help explain the differences in percentages of one-parent families among black poor as compared with those who are white; second, the presence of racial discrimination may help explain why, under favorable economic and family conditions, delinquency rates are higher for Negro than white and not especially higher where both are severely disadvantaged economically and in family circumstances. In the former case, perhaps racism as a variable is more potent.

I think Professor Willie's paper could be more exact in its treatment of white people. Thirteen percent of the white population does mean 23,000,000 people; I doubt that individualization would be an effective approach towards overcoming such poverty. I agree that it might well be less ineffective than with the blacks, since percentages in the latter case are much higher, but Professor Willie's emphasis—perhaps for reasons of ironic commentary—on individualization is perhaps overdone. The likelihood of this is the greater when one observes—and Professor Willie does not do this—that the figure of 13% poor among whites is based on a very minimal income indeed and actually more closely counts not simply the poor among the whites but rather the impoverished.[1] Certainly, it is careless to write—as

[1] In the summer of 1969, the U. S. Government estimated 25.4 million Americans living *below* the poverty line. A Senate report, known as the McGovern report, issued at that time declared that 38 million Americans were existing *below* the poverty line—the first figure was based on a family of three, the second on a family of four.

Professor Willie does—of institutional changes having in fact "prevented poverty among whites" when even the minimum figure does reach a total of twenty-three million human beings!

The main thing about Professor Willie's paper, however, is that it represents a new wind in the sociological literature, particularly in its implicit emphasis upon the ennobling quality of resistance to oppression. I would add that a great need persists for careful examination of the "crippling effect," to quote Andrew Billingsley, of oppression and discrimination and injustice upon those classes and peoples guilty of oppressing, discriminating and (feeling this often in their own innermost hearts) being unjust.[2]

[2] Andrew Billingsley, *Black Families in White America,* p. 68; cf. note 7 in Dr. Willie's paper.

# 3

## THE CULTURE OF POVERTY?
## WHAT DOES IT MATTER?

### HYLAN LEWIS

The title of this paper is not meant to suggest
flippancy toward the idea of a culture of poverty; nor is
it meant to convey despair about the people who are
poor in our society.

In fact, one of my prime aims is to discuss how the
culture of poverty idea does matter: (1) to the
behavioral science disciplines; (2) to the images and life
chances of people, especially the poor; and (3) to the
structuring of relations among individuals and groups. A
second aim is to discuss some of the ways in which the
idea of the culture of poverty and the research methods
associated with it fail to deal with some of the
fundamental human and knowledge issues and often
divert attention from them. In fairness, it is important
to say that some of the reasons why the culture of
poverty idea does not matter as much as it might, have

Copyright © 1969 by Hylan Lewis. Used by permission.

to do more with changes in the community than with the flaws and ventures of a social science concept.

The immediate cues for the title came from three recent observations about the characteristics of poor people. The first came from the anthropologist who coined the term, Oscar Lewis; the second, from a resident of Tarrytown, New York, was a letter to the editor of *The New York Times;* and the third was in the remarks of a black lady from the Washington community who spoke to the psychologists at their recent convention in the capital.

In his recent work, "A Death in the Sanchez Family," Oscar Lewis wrote about Guadalupe, the maternal aunt and closest blood relative of the Sanchez children:

> Although Guadalupe was only a minor character in my book, she played a central role in the Sanchez family. Moreover, she, her husbands, and her neighbors [in the *Vecindad*] were better representatives of the "Culture of Poverty" than were Jesus Sanchez and his children, who were more influenced by Mexican middle-class values and aspirations.[1]

The letter writer from Tarrytown expressed the fears that the proponents of a guaranteed annual income "fail to realize the difference between a poverty income and a poverty culture." He wrote:

> If the income of the culturally poor is raised, they will not suddenly accept the values of the American middle class. Instead, they will merely have more money to spend on the things they always have.
>
> Conversely, graduate students, who must be considered as having a poverty income, are seldom included in discussions about the poor. This is because they lack a poverty culture.

[1] Oscar Lewis, "A Death in the Sanchez Family: A Special Supplement," Part I, *New York Review of Books,* September 11, 1969, p. 3.

(Among other things, the letter writer does not mention the fact that the poverty of the college students is voluntary and temporary under normal circumstances and that it is worn as a badge. The poverty of the bulk of the poor we are talking about is involuntary, and whether it is viewed as deserved or not, it is a stigma.)

The lady from the Washington ghetto told the psychologists: "You psychologists come and tell us that we're uneducable. You people shut up and come to listen to us for a change. If you don't, we're going to shut you out of the ghetto. Fortune tellers, that's all you are—a bunch of fortune tellers."

The statements about the meaning and significance of the culture of poverty, differing as they do, spurred me to examine some of the ways in which the idea of a culture of poverty matters to different segments and interests in our society. The comments of the lady from Washington led me to wonder why the idea of a culture of poverty does not seem to matter, or matters in a negative way, especially with reference to certain kinds of problems and certain kinds of people, notably the poor themselves and blacks and Puerto Ricans.

In the broadest sense, the idea of a culture of poverty matters because its recent flowering and acceptance represent significant developments in the history of social thought, and because it has increasing significance for social structure in our times. It matters because it has become more ideological than scientific. Like the idea of race, the idea of a culture of poverty is an idea that people believe, want to believe, and perhaps need to believe. The belief and its associated assertions and inferences about why some Americans have failed and will continue to fail to make it in the system constitute a reality that matters. Scientific questions aside, this is the important reality that must be dealt with. The idea of a culture of poverty is a fundamental political fact.

There are times when it seems chillingly like the idea of race.

The idea of inherited poverty, as did the idea of race before it, took on new significance as it came to be supported by scientific trappings and the assertions of some behavioral scientists—many engaged in a valid quest for knowledge. Professor Eleanor B. Leacock points out:

> Sociologists and social psychologists have adopted the culture concept from anthropology as helpful in revealing the ways in which social conditions (not innate propensities) lead to differences in group behavior. It is a bitter irony, therefore, that the concept of culture is now being widely applied in such a form as to be almost as pernicious in its application as biological determinist and racist views have been in the past. Through the notion of a "Culture of Poverty," the 19th century argument that poverty is not a socially based problem, but that the poor are poor through their own lack of ability and initiative, has re-entered the scene in a new form, well decked out with scientific jargon and not lacking in scholarly backing.[2]

For these reasons, the culture of poverty idea has significant bearing on the current issues having to do with the pressures and the proposals for political and social reorganization of American society that are based on the imperatives of class and race. It provides assumptions about the enduring characteristics of people and therefore it gives some people important, if not necessarily new, rationales for the reordering of social relationships along both class and racial lines.

Two recent speculative proposals by social scientists —one from a psychologist at the National Institute of Mental Health and the other from a distinguished economist—make projections about the significance for future American social structure of certain dispositions

[2] In the Introduction to the forthcoming *The Culture of Poverty—A Critique* (New York: Simon and Schuster).

74

and abilities of its citizens categorically related to poverty and to race. These intimations of a new quality of class and ethnic pluralism tend to go beyond the important point made by Glazer and Moynihan in *Beyond the Melting Pot* that ethnic groups tend to be political interest groups.

The psychologist in question, Stephen Baratz, made a recent statement at the Center for the Study of Democratic Institutions about his *belief* that there is a unique culture of the black ghetto. His statement is a good example of a kind of hat trick pulled by a person with the credentials of a behavioral scientist. It is based on ambiguous assertions about culture and race and "the black community as it is, not as it is supposed to be."[3] Among other things, he says:

> For the great masses of blacks in our inner-city, the standardized tests of our educational system measure the degree to which they have been *brought* into *our* middle-class life style. The tests reveal nothing about the knowledge and aptitudes of *blacks within their own cultural world* and *their potential or desire* for being absorbed into the mainstream.
>
> I *believe* that a unique culture exists within the ghetto and has persisted from the shores of Africa to Watts and Hough, and Harlem. The *social scientist's denial of this culture,* rather than a lack of understanding of it, has led us down a blind alley. *We have forced the Afro-American into an alien mold* . . . ; because the Afro-American family is not organized in the same way as the idealized white family it is considered disorganized. But it is not that the family is disorganized—it is more accurate to say that it conveys different values to its members. This is the social scientist's hang-up—that he continually compares two different value systems in a way that gives ascendance to one and descendance to another.
>
> The immediate goal of social science should be to

3 Stephen S. Baratz, "The Unique Culture of the Ghetto," *The Center Magazine,* July 1969, p. 28.

determine the cultural strengths of the ghetto, to see how our own style may be in conflict with these strengths, and to develop bridges between these two distinct styles. *Social science needs to make a complete re-evaluation of the assumption on which most of its literature on the Afro-American is based. It needs to return to a form of empirical observation more attuned to the black community as it is, not as it is supposed to be.*

It needs to find a version of acculturation that is recognized as a two-way street between white and black and does not seek to destroy the ties that bind black Americans together.[4]

For its ambiguity, its dissociation of whites from Negroes, and its doubt of the Negro's capacity and ability, Baratz' last paragraph is reminiscent of Thomas Jefferson's letter in 1791 to Benjamin Banneker, the Negro mathematician and astronomer. Banneker had sent Jefferson a copy of his almanac, suggesting that the almanac was evidence of the Negro's ability, and had added some remarks on the injustice of slavery. Jefferson was a complex man who was against slavery in principle, if not in practice; in spite of his benign view, he thought Negroes were not only different but inferior. Jefferson wrote in acknowledgment:

Nobody wishes more than I do to see such proofs as you exhibit, that nature has given to our black brethren, talents equal to those of the other colors of men, and that the appearance of a want of them is owing merely to the degraded condition of their existence, both in Africa and America. I can add with truth, that nobody wishes more ardently to see a good system commenced for raising the condition both of their body and mind to what it ought to be, as fast as the imbecility of their present existence, and other circumstances which cannot be neglected, will admit.[5]

4 *Ibid.,* pp. 27f.; italics added.

5 Quoted in Winthrop D. Jordan, *White Over Black: American Attitudes Toward the Negro, 1550-1812* (Baltimore, Md.: Penguin Books, Inc., 1969), pp. 451f.

Winthrop Jordan observes wryly that Jefferson's letter "was a careful, courteous, and resoundingly ambiguous letter; the condition of the mind and body of the Negro was to be raised 'to what it ought to be.' "[6]

It is important to call attention to the recurrence of the hackneyed plea for realism in looking at the poor and at Negroes. Ambiguous and patronizing references to the black community as it is, not as it is supposed to be, and comments that it might be best to permit it to develop in a way different from the American way, are strangely regressive when they are mouthed by today's social scientists.

The interesting point is that, with some notable exceptions, when representatives of the poor and the blacks refer now to telling it like it is, to having control over their own institutions, and to doing their thing, they don't mean the same things that many representatives of the social sciences and of the middle classes mean when they use the terms. Certainly their versions of the way it ought to be and of taking care of business are not the same either. To say that some blacks are advocating the same thing that Baratz has advocated—separatism—misses the point. Negroes who are given to such positions are talking and acting as politicized blacks: theirs is the rhetoric of politics born of frustration and despair because the American system has not worked for them; and the primary reason it has not worked for them has little to do with their wishes, or their ascribed unique culture, whether it is thought to stem from poverty or from racial experience. Rather, their status and behavior reflect flaws in the American culture and the American experience. The ironic truth is that blacks can neither be written out of this, or withdrawn from it in any effective way, no matter who says they want to, or should be. The issues are sharing

6 *Ibid.,* p. 452.

and the ability to share and the uses of power to affect participation and control.

Baratz' suggestion of the desirability of accepting and encouraging a black ghetto culture essentially follows from his belief that Negroes are not capable or do not want certain things because they have a unique culture. This presumption has been made about no other American citizens.

Taking a slightly different line, more in the nature of musings about the creation of new institutions, the economist Kenneth Boulding speculates about a kind of class pluralism that might be based upon the recognition and acceptance of a poverty substructure and subculture. In a recent book of essays,[7] he points to the problem of "milk and cream," that is, the possible cleavage within and among nations between those who "adapt through education to the world of modern technology" and those who don't make it. He suggests "such a situation [of cleavage] could hardly persist without corrupting the cultures of both the rich and the poor," and that the situation is more serious in other parts of the world than in the United States.

Boulding suggests that major social inventions comparable to such previous ones as the socialist state, banking, insurance, and the corporation, will be necessary in the future. The problem of our times is that these new social inventions now require more rapid development than in the past. He muses that perhaps a society like the United States could afford to abandon its egalitarian, homogenizing pretenses and "invent" a mosaic society of many small subcultures.[8]

These speculations on the future organization of our society and our own reactions to these speculations as

[7] *Beyond Economics: Essays on Society, Religion and Ethics* (Ann Arbor: University of Michigan Press).

[8] Paul Seabury, "Expecting the Worst" (book review), *Science,* April 4, 1969, p. 59.

students and citizens underscore the mixture of reason, politics, and emotion that marks much of our discussion of the poor and of contemporary race relations. Accounts such as these have a chilling effect because they tend to accent institutional contempt for persons; they tend to divert our attention from the demeaning effects of our institutions and from the ways in which many of them betray not only the increasingly self-conscious poor and blacks, but the uneasily affluent and white as well.

These observations about the serious question of alternate systems or of the drastic reorganization of existing systems underscore further the essentially political nature of the question of poverty today and the complexity of the relationships among social science knowledge, political power and social change. They illuminate further the political context in which the idea of a culture of poverty, and the effect on social scientists, must be viewed.

A 1969 report of the Special Commission on the Social Sciences of the National Science Foundation makes two interrelated points on social science, politics, and vested interests. First, "social change—whether arising from social science knowledge or from some other source—threatens to erode the political power of one or another individual or group not interested in sharing or giving up the political position already held" (p. 19). Second, "whether or not the nation will use the social sciences in a given instance depends upon the outcome of the political competition among different vested interests with all their degrees of approval and disapproval toward any matter at issue" (p. 19).

Many groups have both political and scientific stakes in the idea of a culture of poverty. The idea matters a great deal to the behavioral science disciplines, taken separately and together—anthropology, sociology, psychology, economics, political science and, given the new interest in genetics, to biology. The idea is a prime test of their theories, their methods, and rightly or wrongly, their pertinence and credibility. In comparable ways the idea matters to the applied disciplines concerned with health, education, welfare, communications, policy and planning, and the various approaches to conflict resolution. The idea is a prime test of their ability to provide and plan essential services.

The idea matters also to the groups of scholars and researchers who have invested their energies and reputations in efforts to establish the primacy and the validity of views of the culture of poverty. Similarly, it matters to persons in applied fields and in policy-making positions who are shopping for ideas, but are primarily interested in the usefulness of the idea.

A chief practical contribution of social science writings and research on the culture of poverty has come from the way in which they have helped force and have facilitated a focusing on the serious problems of poverty and racism. This effect has had no necessary relationship to the scientific validity of the findings or to any social science consensus. It may be a sign of a basic strain toward sanity and health that the concept has had its greatest circulation at the same time that the serious questioning of the relevance of the social sciences to the problems of poverty and racism was accelerating.

This questioning of the social sciences may be related to what S. M. Miller has pointed out, that for many years the social sciences and the general public have ignored or discounted the effects on our society of the continued blunting of black political participation, of the failure of professional services, and of the effects of new transformations and redefinitions of power and income that are occurring in our society.

The idea of the culture of poverty is an example of a major social science idea and preoccupation that has contributed its part to the increasing estrangement of the poor, the black, and the youth from old-line intellectuals and established men of science. The credibility, the relevance, the politics, and the humanity of scientists are being questioned by the poor, the black, and the youths. Although the idea of the culture of poverty has helped focus on the problem of the poor in our society, the effect of some of its versions and uses has been to divert energies and attention from the need for significant changes in the educational, occupational, and political structures. It has had the effect of helping to divert attention from the critical crunches in our society related to the fact that new generations—of black youths, black lower and middle classes, and youths—are "seeking for power [and radical change now] as against an older generation [and other ethnics] satisfied with just a little more opportunity."[9]

Professor David Eaton, in his presidential address to the recent annual meeting of the American Political Science Association, pointed out that in recent years "the talents of political scientists have been put in the service largely the elites in society—in government, business, the military and voluntary organizations." Further, "the professional is seen as having little communication and contact with those who characteristically benefit least from the fruits of modern industrial society—the racial and economic minorities, the unrepresented publics at home, and the colonial masses abroad."

> One factor is also clear. The crisis of our times spares no group, not even the social sciences. The pressures to utilize all of our resources in critically evaluating goals as well as in providing effective means are too great to be denied. For increasing numbers of us, it is no longer practical or morally

[9] Nicolaus C. Mills, "Black Youth and the NAACP," *Dissent,* July-August 1969, p. 300.

tolerable to stand on the political sidelines when our expertise alerts us to disaster.[10]

Many students would agree with Bernard Pyron that "the problem of effectively reducing economic deprivation in America is in large part related to the perception of the poor by the non-poor," and that "it is also a problem involving the values which determine the perception of the poor by the non-poor. For it is the representatives of the majority of the non-poor who decide whether or not to make effective use of current proposals to reduce economic deprivation."[11]

The acceptance and the workings of income maintenance programs and job training programs as features of employment and income strategies, for example, are affected by the perceptions of the poor by the nonpoor.

> Giving money to the poor on a non-contingent basis or for governmental support of on-the-job-training or work created by the federal government contradicts the prime American value which says that one should earn money in direct proportion to the effort he expends in working within the capitalistic labor market (exchange justice). An alternative value says that the *responsibility* for providing the necessities of life for the twenty to thirty percent of the population who are defined as poor is an obligation of society through government. The problem is whether America was to invest $15 to $30 billion a year to reduce economic deprivation. Thus, an over-riding problem for all employment and income strategies is to change the negative perceptions of many of the non-poor toward the poor . . . .[12]

Pyron goes on to hypothesize about the effect of perceptions of the poor:

[10] Quoted in *The New York Times,* September 8, 1969, p. 47.

[11] Bernard Pyron, "The Perception of the Poor by the Non-poor" (mimeographed paper).

[12] *Ibid.*

The non-poor who hold strongly to exchange justice would ... feel that there is an inequity in giving monetary rewards to the poor when they expend little or no effort to justify the rewards. Those who hold to the value of [societal] responsibility would be able to justify giving money to people who are below the poverty line.

The non-poor who believe in exchange justice and feel that the poor do not deserve outcomes greater than their inputs ... tend to generate negative feeling toward the poor.... Given that a middle-class person has a general negative feeling toward the poor, one way for him to maintain consistency within his perceptual and belief systems is to assume that the poor have a whole cluster of inter-related negative character traits. The non-poor person who believes in exchange justice would perceive that the poor are economically deprived because they have defective character, are lazy or lack initiative. Even professional social workers have tended to associate with economic deprivation a cluster of negative traits.

The belief in exchange justice may have also motivated some social scientists to search for basic sociological, cultural and psychological homogeneity in the poor....

The data on the number of families on general relief in 1961 and in 1966, also disconfirm the view that poverty is largely determined by negative personality traits which make a person unemployable. In March, 1961, at the depth of the recession period, there were 525,000 families on general relief and in January, 1966, there were less than 300,000 families on general relief. This drop indicated that many of the men on relief were employable and were willing to find work if the work existed.[13]

There are other points that might be made in this connection about the relationship between employment and poverty and the behavior of people who are poor. One is that the employment level and, consequently, the number of persons who are poor at any one time are in a basic sense functions of federal economic policies. For example, on October 7, 1969, Secretary of the Treasury

[13] *Ibid.*

Kennedy told Congress that a four percent unemployment rate was "acceptable" to the administration and
that the administration believed it was necessary to
continue policies that might force unemployment even
higher. He added, when pressed, that he could not give a
figure to identify the highest unemployment rate the
administration would consider acceptable.

A second group of observations about employment
and poverty concerns the earning differentials between
whites and blacks, and the significance of continuing
discrimination by employers and unions.

Of the more than 25.2 million people classified as
poor in the United States, only about one in seven is out
of a job. Six million of the poor work fulltime,
year-round, at jobs which do not pay a living wage. The
August 1969 Census Reports show further that one-
third of Negroes are categorized as poor; this represents
a drop from 56 percent in 1951 to 33 percent in 1968.
For the nation as a whole, the number categorized as
poor is just under one in seven. This represents a drop
from 22 percent in 1961 to 13 percent in 1968. It
would be difficult to attribute any signficant part of this
decrease to the government's poverty program or to
changes in values of the poor.

Herman Miller has shown that the gap between black
and white earnings has not changed essentially over the
last twenty years, despite increases in real wages for
both groups, and he shows further that the gap between
black and white income is relatively greater when
education is controlled: the average nonwhite person
with four years of college can expect to earn less over a
lifetime than the white who did not go beyond the
eighth grade. This persistent gap is an external fact that
undoubtedly has some effect upon motivations. Further, there are important consequences of the type of
labor market behavior that sees people with inadequate
and marginal incomes seeking to raise family income by

holding more than one job, working more hours and having other family members seek employment.

A Harvard University study reported in April 1969 that the black returns to education are much lower than the returns for whites, even when we correct for the blacks' lower average level of learning.[14]

Current programs place a great deal of stress on the need for the disadvantaged to upgrade job skills. However, there are some students, such as Ivar Berg and Shirley Gorelick, who stress that an argument can be made for the crucial role of employer policies in creating or thwarting opportunities. They charge that credentialism and educational qualifications are used for enlarging employers' and medium and top level employees' gains at the expense of the less educated.

A part of the argument holds that (1) many jobs do not need for their performance the level of "talent" required to obtain them, and (2) that the "talents" needed are not so scarce among the population as many persons have been led to believe. The argument goes:

> The practice of linking jobs to education levels results in the denial of higher level jobs to the less educated for these reasons:
>
> (1) It arbitrarily lessens the number of people qualified to do the higher level jobs. By so restricting this pool the average wage or salary is made to be higher than it would otherwise be; and (2) exclusion of the less educated from these jobs arbitrarily increases the pool of people for lower jobs.
>
> Insofar as the bulk of the wage pool comes from lower level jobs . . . the discrimination by education is profitable.

Shirley Gorelick argues that in the labor market "blatant racism has become somewhat muted and a more justifiable and seemingly neutral principle has

---

[14] Harvard University Program on Regional and Urban Economics, "The Effects of Education on the Earnings of Blacks and Whites" (mimeographed), p. 21.

taken the place of overt racism in keeping blacks expanding competition for the lowest level jobs. That principle has been education." She suggests that:

> In the tug of war over lower level wage rates the efforts of employers to keep wages low and of unions to raise them cumulate to disadvantaged blacks. Employers use various exclusionary screening principles which may or may not be racist in form but whose effect is to make large numbers of blacks either unemployed or available for low level jobs. White unions, seeking to restrict the pool of labor available in order to be able to demand wage increases, seek to exclude blacks either indirectly through nepotism rules and apprenticeship tests, or more directly and blatantly. The consequences are heavy black unemployment and heavy black concentration in lower paying jobs.[15]

The idea of a culture of poverty matters most to the poor. Because of its vogue they have had and will have labels placed on their capacities, their needs, and their preferences. These labels are used by people who make decisions that are critical with reference to the amount and the distribution of the essential services that affect their educational and employment opportunities, their housing and their health.

This happens and will continue to happen without any necessary relationship to the quality of research on the culture of poverty hypothesis; and the fact that it will occur does not mean that there should be a moratorium or cessation of research on poverty. On the contrary, the flap should signal the need for more significant studies of the nexus between poverty and affluence. There should be especially more research that seeks to get the perspectives and the participation of more of the blacks and the poor; that seeks to develop more and better systems of delivery for essential health

---

[15] This quotation and this whole section are based upon an unpublished proposal, "Incentives and Obstacles to Management Hiring of the Disadvantaged."

and welfare services; that seeks to discover ways to cope with and manage the information explosion, the prodigious growth of scientific knowledge and the increasing fragmentation of that knowledge.

The following is a grim fact and a statistic that should help put in proper perspective much of the discussion about the etiology of poverty and the role of the culture of poverty:

> Surely everyone can agree that science has done wonderful things for the improvement of health. But, even here, uncomfortable questions are being asked. Have our best doctors become so preoccupied with the wonders of their technology that they have become indifferent to the plight of large numbers of people who suffer from conditions just as fatal but much less interesting? Even the most earnest advocates of increased research in heart disease, cancer, and stroke must be a little bit embarrassed by the fact that the United States, which used to be a world leader in reducing infant mortality rates, has now fallen to 15th place.[16]

My own view is that the most important research in this area now should focus not on the culture of poverty but on the culture of affluence—this is the culture that matters more and that is far more dangerous than the culture of poverty. Jean Mayer has put the thrust and the focus succinctly:

> There is a strong case to be made for a stringent population policy on exactly the reverse of the basis Malthus expounded. Malthus was concerned with the steadily more widespread poverty that indefinite population growth would inevitably create. I am concerned about the areas of the globe where people are rapidly becoming richer. For rich people occupy much more space, consume more of each natural resource, disturb the ecology more, and create more land, air, water, chemical, thermal, and radioactive pollution than poor people. So it can be argued that from

[16] Robert S. Morison, "Science and Social Attitudes," *Science,* CLXV (July 11, 1969), 152.

many viewpoints it is even more urgent to control the numbers of the rich than it is to control the numbers of the poor.[17]

The primary concern of this paper has not been to examine the scientific significance of the culture of poverty concept, for the concept has been examined and assessed by a number of students, including myself, and most thoroughly and brilliantly recently by Charles Valentine, and many others including Camille Jeffers, Elliot Liebow, Lee Rainwater, Dorothy Newman, Elizabeth Herzog, Kenneth Clark, Eleanor Leacock; and its scientific significance as such is only one of the things that matters mightily today.

In thinking about this paper, I thought back over some observations I made as far back as 1960 in connection with a study of low income families in Washington, D. C. I would like to close with a paraphrase of some of my observations that appear to be still pertinent to questions raised about the way in which the culture of poverty matters to science, public policy, and to the people who are affluent as well as poor.[18]

(1) Many of the formulations of lower-class culture, as well as of the culture of poverty, with which it is frequently confused, contain within them a number of intellectual assumptions and untested hypotheses. These

[17] Jean Mayer, "Toward a Non-Malthusian Population Policy," *Columbia Forum,* Summer 1969, p. 5.

[18] The observations that follow are from Hylan Lewis, "Child Rearing Practices Among Low-Income Families in the District of Columbia: A Progress Report," March 1961, mimeographed; "Child Rearing Practices Among Low-Income Families in the District of Columbia," adapted from a paper presented at the National Conference on Social Welfare, May 16, 1961, Minneapolis; "Culture, Class and the Behavior of Low-Income Families," adapted from a paper presented at the Conference on Lower Class Culture, June 27-29, 1963, New York City, revised August, 1965; "The Culture of Poverty Approach to Social Problems," adapted from a paper delivered at the Plenary Session of the Annual Meeting of the Society for the Study of Social Problems, August 29, 1964, Montreal. The last three are included in Lewis, *Culture, Class and Poverty.*

often beget generalizations that are not consonant with existing data. For these reasons, it is urgent that the versions of lower-class culture and of the culture of poverty that have filtered into pedagogical and social welfare planning and practice and popular thinking should be looked at very carefully.

(2) One danger lies in the tendency to subsume under the term lower-class culture a medley of traits without making distinctions among the kinds of traits and among levels of abstraction. A related danger comes from the failure to separate essence from accident, the crucial from the trivial, and the persistent from the transitory in the packages of traits.

(3) The behaviors observed in the bulk of poor families are not generated by or guided by an urban lower-class "cultural system in its own right—with an integrity of its own." This is not meant to suggest that there are no differences other than income between this category and the adequate income category of the population, or that there are no modalities in the characteristics and in the behaviors of the poor. There are several modes of styles of low income (and lower-class) living rather than a single or basic mode or style. We are impressed by the range and variability of structures and behaviors within the low income category.

(4) There are significant differences in hopes and expectations here of changes for the better, and in the estimates of resources poor parents think they have or can find to effect changes in themselves. In other words, there are cutting points in the optimism and confidence of many parents about the futures of their families and in the belief that their efforts alone might affect them.

(5) Confidence that is continuing—even though mixed or fluctuating—as much as anything distinguishes low income families that are not now marked by neglect or

dependency from those that are "clinically" dependent or neglectful.

(6) The "multi-problem" or "hard core" cases of inadequacy, dependency and neglect are, to use medical terminology, "clinical cases" with unknown or varying potential for rehabilitation. As in types of heart disease and cancer, when the condition becomes known or public, it is frequently too late; prognosis for these relatively few cases is poor. "Clinical" dependency—that which is known to public and private agencies and health and welfare institutions—is costly and provokes concern beyond the numbers involved. And, although it is necessary and important to seek improved ways of rehabilitation or containment, the long-range dividends are likely to be greater from research and demonstration programs that seek to identify and work with the highly vulnerable families, not yet publicly dependent or neglectful—to examine the "preclinical" and "subclinical" aspects of dependency and neglect.

(7) The behaviors of the bulk of the low income families appear as pragmatic adjustments to external and internal stresses and deprivations experienced in the quest for essentially common values. A seeming paradox is that affirmation of, if not demonstration of, some of America's traditional virtues and values in their purest form is found to be strong and recurrent among even the most deprived.

(8) It is more fruitful to think of different types of lower-class families reacting in various ways to the facts of their position and to relative isolation rather than to the imperatives of lower-class culture.

(9) It is important not to confuse basic life chances and actual behavior with basic cultural values and preferences.

(10) Many of the urban poor straddle poverty and affluence. They may exhibit complex and fluctuating

HYLAN LEWIS

mixtures of the living situations and styles, possessions and tastes of different consumption levels and classes.

(11) The focus of efforts to change aspects of the behavior of people should be on background conditions and on precipitants of the significantly deviant behaviors, rather than on presumably different class or cultural values.

(12) The family environment of a poor family may fluctuate markedly over relatively brief periods of child rearing time.

(13) It is not likely that the way to remove the threat and to reduce the costs of deviant aspects of the behavior of poor or lower-class people—or rather segments of the poor and lower class that threaten and cost most at this time—is to be found in direct efforts to change a lower-class culture or a culture of poverty that is perceived as significantly different and alien. Significant change is not likely to come from efforts that add up to indulging, or to sealing off, or to trying to get lower-class people themselves to revamp what is presumed to be their unique culture. There is danger that the concept will encourage the development of a spurious cultural relativism based upon race and class.

(14) The concept lower-class culture has valid but limited uses in tackling contemporary problems of dependency, delinquency, crime, and mental health. However, the fact that the concept is valid, and perhaps necessary, for research and theory purposes—and for use on certain levels—does not mean necessarily that in its present form it should be either the appropriate or decisive guide to policy and programming. It certainly is not the most useful single tool to place in the hands of those who deal directly with poor people who have problems.

(15) The lower income male and father is a key figure in gaining an understanding of child rearing in the poor or dependent family. Of particular importance is the

man's ability to support and stand for the family—to play the economic and social roles wished of him, particularly by wives, mothers, and children. Some of the implications of this are suggested in the field document that describes a mother of six children chiding her husband for being afraid and not showing aggressiveness in looking for a second job to increase the family income. Showing his pay stub, she said: "This looks like a receipt for a woman's paycheck instead of a man's."

One of the significant differences between 1960 and today is the pervasive force of a highly politicized black consciousness. Although the responses of the Negro/black, poor and nonpoor to heightened black consciousness are not to be described simplistically, the dramatic quality of affirmation, protest, and assertiveness—traits that have never been absent—now tends to dwarf, if not to dispute categorically, the force of a culture of poverty among Negroes.

Even before the recent surge of race and class consciousness, the evidence is that Negroes and the poor tended to react negatively to the label and the implications of the culture of poverty when they were made aware of it and felt its invidious consequences. This is only one of the prime reasons questions will be raised continually about the concept; and that there will be indications that the idea of a culture of poverty matters less as a useful guide to conflict resolution based on economic deprivation and color, to positive social change, and to needed institutional alternatives in our society—whether that society is black and white, integrated or not. The paradox is that the black power movement in interesting ways has reduced, if not destroyed, the power of the idea of the culture of poverty as a scientific explanatory variable at the same time that it has increased its force as a political idea—an ideology. And this is why it matters.

# COMMENTS ON "THE CULTURE OF POVERTY? WHAT DOES IT MATTER?"

## ARTHUR SHOSTAK

Let us be clear from the outset about my conception of my role. In 1964, when I began to co-edit the first paperback anthology on the "War on Poverty,"[1] I asked specialists for the name of someone who could help me understand the even-then controversial concept of the "culture of poverty." Hylan Lewis was the man most often cited, and I journeyed to his Health and Welfare Council office in the District of Columbia, and "sat at his feet." Busy as he was he made time for me, and shared with me a pile of unpublished "culture" essays that he had no time to polish for publication.

Those essays of Hylan's were strong and insightful; the essay in this volume is no less so, and is still more thoroughgoing and significant. So, I write not as an antagonist or literary critic. Rather, I write as a long-time student of Hylan Lewis, as one deeply appreciative of his pioneering efforts where our subject—"the culture of poverty"—is concerned.

This is not to say that Hylan and I do not have our differences in this matter. I said "student," not slavish adherent. We had our differences concerning the concept five years ago, and have them still today. So, in the spirit of the constructive criticism that we owe one another as professionals, as academics, and, even the more so, as personal friends, I urge the following five changes on Hylan:

1. *More Use of Citation.* Many have joined Hylan

[1] A. Shostak and W. Gomberg, eds., *New Perspectives on Poverty* (Englewood Cliffs, N.J.: Prentice-Hall, 1964).

Lewis in condemning the misuse of the "culture of poverty" concept and the abuses committed in its name. In his paper, for example, he writes,

> Although the idea of the culture of poverty has helped focus on the problem of the poor in the society, the effect of some of its versions and uses has been to divert energies and attention from the need for significant changes in the educational, occupational, and political structure.

But to what "versions and uses" is Hylan specifically referring? This we never learn. It may safely be assumed that Daniel Patrick Moynihan's Negro Family essay, the writings of Oscar Lewis, and perhaps even the early essays of Walter B. Miller earn Hylan's censure, but nowhere does he—nor do other critics of the "culture" concept—clearly say. It is well past the time for conventional niceties, and it is vital now to name the names, the better that we outside the dispute might judge it.

2. *More Use of Example.* Again, I come back to the heart of Hylan Lewis' case, the alleged abuses committed in the name of the "culture of poverty" concept. Unfortunately, he cites no specific example. Overdue is the proof or line of reasoning by Hylan and like-minded others that demonstrates the damage done to any one or several anti-poverty efforts—what CAP has the concept harmed? Get Set program? Foster Grandparent effort? This is far from clear, regardless of how strongly it is contended. And the issue *per se* is provocatively illuminated by the failure of the first book-length evaluation of the "War on Poverty" to mention the culture concept even once in its 318 pages.[2]

3. *More Use of Refinement.* It is saddening to participate in the conference deliberations and find in them little more conceptual rigor and refinement than

[2] Sar Levitan, *The Great Society's Poor Law* (Baltimore: Johns Hopkins Press, 1969).

was available five years ago when conference-goers like ourselves first "rediscovered" poverty. In particular it is dismaying to note the singular referent that lurks behind many uses made of the "culture of poverty" concept. It is as if we had a formula which read: *one body of poor Americans equals one culture of poverty.* Hylan goes past this point far too quickly when he observes, only in passing, that "there are several modes of styles of low income (and lower class) living rather than a single or basic mode or style." Here is his most telling criticism of the "culture concept," and he does far too little with it.

Relevant in this regard are these thoughts from William Yancey, a sociologist who did extensive research in the Pruitt-Igoe housing project in St. Louis:

> Immediately after we characterize the lower class by the culture of poverty we must add a second generalization: that there is more within-group variation among the lower class than in any other stratum in American society. In other words, it is more difficult to predict the behavior of a lower class person than that of a person in the middle, working, or upper class. . . .[3]

Relevant also is the typology advanced five years ago by S. M. Miller, which delineates four distinct "cultures" among the poor (that of the Stable, Copers, Skidders, and Unstable), and thereby helps free us of the fallacy of the single referent.[4] Hylan could—and should—help us all learn how to "grow up" beyond our current monocentric abuse of the "culture" concept.

4. *Less Use of False Comparison.* In the place of the usual call for more research on the topic Hylan substitutes a more provocative call for the redirection of

---

[3] William L. Yancey (Washington University, St. Louis), "The Culture of Poverty: Not So Much Parsimony" (unpublished undated paper), pp. 4f.

[4] "The American Lower Classes: A Typological Approach," in A. Shostak and W. Gomberg, eds., *Blue-Collar World* (Englewood Cliffs: Prentice-Hall, 1964), pp. 9-23.

research elsewhere: " . . . the most important research in this area now should focus not on the culture of poverty, but on the culture of affluence that matters more and that is far more dangerous than the culture of poverty."

Clearly we need more research both on poverty *and* affluence. It is misleading to insist one is "more dangerous" than the other without specifying how, for what, and why, all of which is possibly unavailable given the alleged lack of adequate research to date. It is misleading to suggest without further clarification that one matters more than the other.[5] Above all, it is misleading to urge a switch away from research on a body of Americans known only too recently as "invisible" in favor of a larger body of Americans discussed in the research essays of every issue of every social science journal.

There is ominous reason to already suspect that research on poverty is fading as a typical interest of faddish social scientists (compare the indexes of journals in this matter for 1964 and 1969). It is doubly unfortunate, therefore, to find a poverty researcher of the competence and renown of Hylan Lewis urging his colleagues to invest scarce research resources elsewhere.

5. *More Attention to Academic Malfeasance.* Recognizing the considerable merit in Hylan Lewis' indictment of some misuses of the "culture of poverty" concept one is left with the unsettling question —"why?" Nowhere does he offer any explanation for academic malfeasance in the matter, and he thereby lets our profession off far too easily.

If conferences like this suggest anything they suggest

---

[5] Excellent in this respect is Harry C. Bredemaier, "The Politics of Poverty," *Urban Affairs Quarterly,* June 1968. See also Arthur B. Shostak, "The Forgotten Man and the Institutions of Government" in *Staff Report, Law and Order* (Washington: Government Printing Office, 1969). (President's Commission on the Causes of Crime and Violence.)

to me the existence of a culture of (education) poverty! It is increasingly apparent that much is wrong in *our* state of Denmark, that our graduate training does not train, our journals do not communicate, our research does not earn replication and enhancement, our conceptual advances do not earn circulation and adoption, and our profession does not professionally advance. The sorry state of today's (1969) discussion of the old "culture of poverty" concept bears witness to and is a victim of this hapless matter.

Hylan Lewis should "tell it like it is"! The culture concept has been abused largely because our house is not in order; the concept is victimized by the half-baked nature of the contemporary social sciences. We must reform our training, our journals, our research, our cross-fertilization, and our mission in general, or come endlessly to conferences like this for public confessionals, and rank demonstrations of our many academic shortcomings. Hylan Lewis can—and should—take more of the lead in this vital matter.

So much for our differences—Hylan and me—and so much more for our common agreements. I came as his student, and leave as his student, more knowledgeable for having heard him, and stronger for knowing how well and wisely he has heard me engage now with him.

# 4

## SUBCULTURE AND SOCIAL REFORM: THE CASE OF "THE CULTURE OF POVERTY"

### WALTER B. MILLER

The circumstances of persons at lower social-status levels in the United States have assumed enormous importance in recent years. The life conditions and customary pursuits of those in the lowest educational, occupational, and income categories lie close to the core of many if not most of the major domestic issues of the past decade—issues tagged with terms such as the urban crisis, the mess of public welfare, the crisis in education, the black revolution, the white backlash, a culture of violence, crime in the streets. These developments have thrown into sharp relief a long-term failure of our society: our inability to develop generally acceptable terms of reference for low-status populations or to reach any substantial degree of agreement as to how to define or characterize this sector of our society.

This failure in large part accounts for the vagueness, ambiguity, and overlap in terms used both by professionals and the lay public, and for rapid and often puzzling shifts in terminological fashion. A bewildering confusion of terms such as the "working class," the "poor," the "working poor," the "black poor," the "white poor," the "underprivileged," the "culturally deprived," the "minorities," the "underclass," move in and out of fashion, with their scope and objects of reference shifting, expanding and contracting to apply to different sectors of different populations at different times. Failures in national policy with respect to the social problems of low-status populations are intimately related to failures in developing adequate modes of conceptualization.

Faced with urgent domestic problems in the 1960's, many of them related directly or indirectly to the massive migrations during and after World War II of low-status southern blacks into northern cities, policymakers at all levels of government—federal, state, and local—were confronted with the pressing need to develop policies of sufficient scope and sweep to match the scope and sweep of cities in flames, violent protest demonstrations, and the growing popularity of a philosophy of revolution among the rising class of black intellectuals. In a desperate search for general guidelines in this complex area, federal policymakers came upon a conceptual model developed in the early 1960's by Oscar Lewis—a cultural anthropologist with a background in Spanish-American ethnography. This model, popularized under the term "the culture of poverty," played a major role, although by no means the only role, in the thinking of those who formulated the "war on poverty" of the Kennedy-Johnson administrations. While many who used it interpreted the concept quite differently from the way Lewis intended, there is no gainsaying that it exerted considerable influence, however understood, on federal policy.

The "culture of poverty" concept, in brief, centers on

the notion that certain low-status populations, in Spanish America and elsewhere, manifest a particular set of characteristics that are closely related to their position in the social order and the role they play in that order, that these characteristics show a fairly high degree of mutual cohesion, and that they tend to endure over time through normal processes of cultural transmission.[1] Stated in this very general form, there seems to be nothing very controversial about this thesis, but in fact it aroused violent opposition, and became embroiled in a series of disputes that often gave Lewis the feeling of being an embattled defender of a misunderstood cause.

At the risk of considerable oversimplification, one can picture Lewis and his culture of poverty concept as fighting three different battles on three different battlefields. Not only were weapons, adversaries, and tactics different in each, but it was often difficult to tell on which of these battlefields an individual engagement was occurring. On the first battlefield the major adversaries were most politicians and their constituencies versus most social scientists, and the issue was essentially that of social classes versus no social classes. The culture of poverty concept implies the existence in the United States and elsewhere of well-developed and relatively stable social classes, differing not only in income but in

[1] The great bulk of Lewis' published work dealing with low-status populations consists of autobiographical accounts by individual informants, taped and edited. However, statements on a more general or theoretical level do appear in several places in his works. Among these are the introduction to *The Children of Sanchez,* pp. xi-xxxi, and a section of the introduction to *La Vida* entitled "The Culture of Poverty," pp. xlii-lii. Another version of this statement appears in "The Culture of Poverty," *Scientific American,* CCXV, No. 4 (October, 1966), 19-24. A third version, also entitled "The Culture of Poverty" appears as Chapter 7 of D. P. Moynihan, ed., *On Understanding Poverty: Perspectives from the Social Sciences* (New York: Basic Books, 1968), pp. 188-199, which in turn is taken from Lewis' *The Study of Slum Culture: Backgrounds for La Vida* (New York: Random House, 1968).

101

life-style as well—a notion that many have been extremely reluctant to accept.

On the second battleground both adversaries were social scientists—anthropologically oriented on the one side versus sociologically and economically oriented on the other. Most social scientists accept the notion of social classes in some form or other, but dispute intensely and often acrimoniously as to how they are to be conceptualized, what their defining criteria should be, how stable they are, and the scope of behavior affected by class-related factors.

One of the major disputes in this arena concerns the extent to which something called "social classes," however defined, can be credited with something called "culture," however defined. Many sociologists and economists concede the utility of conceiving societies as a set of classes or strata to which one may assign different values relating to readily quantifiable characteristics such as income, years of education, rent payment, and the like, but balk at the notion that along with these numerical bases of differentiation there may also go organized and persisting styles of life that have a direct and systematic effect on values, outlook, customary behavioral practices, expenditure preferences, and the like. The issue of how persistent classes are and the degree to which class cultures are transmitted through time are also central points of contention.[2]

The third battle is part of an internecine war among anthropologists themselves. Most of these accept the notion that large industrialized societies can profitably be conceived as comprising a set of differentiated

[2] Different viewpoints respecting this issue are presented in Moynihan *op. cit.,* by Herbert J. Gans ("Class and Culture in the Study of Poverty: An Approach to Anti-poverty Research," pp. 201-228), Lee Rainwater ("The Problem of Lower Class Culture and Poverty-war Strategy, pp. 229-259), and Walter B. Miller ("The Elimination of the American Lower Class as Federal Policy: A Critique of the Ideology of the Poverty Movement of the 1960's," pp. 260-315).

classes, and that such classes generally show sufficient variation from the national culture of which they are a part so that one can speak of "subcultures"—some of whose characteristics are common to all classes, and others of which differ in form, scale, weighting, or patterning. The dispute here concerns the way that class subcultures should be conceptualized, and in some cases whether they should be conceptualized at all. The present paper, as part of this intra-anthropological controversy, examines what the author sees as two major defects in the culture of poverty concept as formulated to date by Oscar Lewis. These are, first, its *conceptual inadequacy*—that is, its failure to provide the basis for a generally applicable and logically consistent theoretical model of culture and subculture—and second, its *normative inadequacy*—its incorporation on an inconsistent and unsystematic basis of a particular set of largely unexamined value premises.

With respect to conceptual adequacy, it should be pointed out that a direct or point-by-point critique of the Lewis formulation will not be presented here, since a fair number of such critiques are already available. This paper presents very briefly an outline of a subcultural approach that may be seen as embodying some of the elements of general applicability and theoretical adequacy that Lewis' formulation lacks, with the hope that the differences between the two will serve to clarify the character of both. It is important to note here that Lewis makes no claim to have developed a comprehensive theoretical system but instead regards the culture of poverty concept as a "challenging hypothesis." In this connection it should be remarked that the task of developing a general explanational system based on the concept of subculture—analogous, say, to the Freudian or psychodynamic system—presents formidable difficulties, and present formulations are still in a very primitive stage. The formulations presented here have been selected and condensed from a detailed theoretical examination by the author of the relations of subculture and customary behavior, which, although quite comprehensive, has still failed to solve some rather serious analytic problems.[3]

Before undertaking the discussion of what appears to the author to be a more adequate theoretical formulation, it is important to specify the objective, for present purposes, of such an endeavor. It is clear that a formulation that is quite adequate for one set of purposes may be quite inadequate for others, and later sections will attempt to show that one difficulty with Lewis' formulations is that they are trying to combine several sets of purposes that articulate poorly with one another. The primary purpose in the present context is that of using the concept of subculture to develop as adequate as possible an *explanation of customary forms of behavioral practice* of specified categories of persons. There is no intention of conveying approval or disapproval of these forms, nor suggesting which should be changed and which should not. It is the classic scholarly objective of *maximum explanational adequacy.* In this context the category of persons for whose behavior an explanation is sought may be called the *low-skilled laboring class.*[4]

Note several things about this term. First, it refers to a designated category of persons, and not to a feature or features of a style of life. Second, it centers on the term

---

[3] Walter B. Miller, "Subculture and Customary Behavior." Report submitted to National Institute of Mental Health, U. S. Public Health Service, January, 1965 (76 pages).

[4] See Walter B. Miller, in Moynihan, *op. cit.,* p. 260, for a discussion of the subculture of low-skilled labor in the United States. The term "lower-class III" is used to refer to the indicated population in W. B. Miller, "Violent Crimes in City Gangs," *Annals of the American Academy of Political and Social Science,* 343 (March, 1966), 99. Definitions appear in W. B. Miller, "An Urban Lower Class Community," in S. M. Miller and S. M. Lipset, *Poverty and Social Stratification* (in preparation).

"subculture" rather than "culture." Third, it contains the term "class" but not the term "poverty." I would like to make it quite clear that although the term "culture of poverty" appears in the subtitle of this paper, I do not find that concept a useful one, and do not use it in my thinking or writing. The concept I do use, the "subculture of the low-skilled laboring class" (in more technical usages the "lower-class III subculture"), refers to a population that overlaps to a considerable degree with that which concerns Lewis, but is far from identical with it. For example, while few persons in this category have much money in the long run, some have fair amounts from time to time, and many live under circumstances quite different from what is referred to as desperate poverty. In addition, in the United States, this category does not include the approximately 50% of those with annual incomes under $3,000 who get their money from interest, royalties, dividends, pensions, and the like, and who are generally included in government statistics on the size of the "poverty" population.[5] Lewis, it should be noted, is quite aware of this problem, and tries to accommodate it by his distinction between "poverty" and a "culture of poverty."[6]

In using the concept of "subculture" for purposes of explanation, it is most important to make every effort to minimize the tautology to which the subcultural mode of analysis is vulnerable. For example, formulations have been forwarded along these lines: "The behavior of youth who commit crimes may be called a delinquency subculture; being in a delinquency subculture causes youth to commit crimes"; or "The way of life of poor people may be called a culture of poverty; being caught in a culture of poverty is the reason that

[5] Herman P. Miller, *Income Distribution in the United States* (Washington: Government Printing Office, 1966), esp. Tables 2-3, page 43.

[6] Oscar Lewis, *La Vida,* p. xlviii, and in *Scientific American,* p. 23.

people are poor." Statements in this form or in more complex forms that can be reduced to this form are one reason that the subcultural framework is in poor repute among many social scientists. Since subculture as a construct is ultimately based on behavior, the logical circularity involved in explaining behavior by behavior is difficult, perhaps impossible, to avoid entirely. What is feasible is a continuing attempt to make this explanational framework *as free as possible* from the more obvious forms of circular reasoning. Some tautology will always remain, but the test of explanational adequacy lies in whether the mode of explanation, whatever degree of tautology it may embody, can cast light on the nature and origins of behavioral phenomena that otherwise appear obscure or are less-well-explained in other frames of reference.

One of the major ways of attempting to reduce tautology is by making as clear as possible a conceptual distinction between two things: a designated population of individuals, on the one hand, and a designated set of behavioral practices and conceptions of appropriate practice on the other. The term "status class" is used here to refer to the first, and "subculture" to refer to the second.[7] Maintaining the distinction between a designated category of persons and the things they do or think helps both to reduce tautology and to avoid a second major defect in the way "subculture" is often used. One selects a behavioral practice or general condition—very often one of which one doesn't approve—and tags the word "subculture" on to it. Thus we have the culture or subculture of violence, of delinquency, of poverty, of bombing, of apathy. Such usage is *ad hoc,* unsystematic, and essentially arbitrary. There are no criteria for specifying what should legitimately be considered a subculture and what should not, and almost limitless

[7] W. B. Miller, "Subculture and Customary Behavior," p. 24 *passim.*

freedom to characterize just about anything as a subculture. For purpose of explanational adequacy, all entities designated as "subcultures" should have significant common properties, and should be defined within a systematic definitional framework. Moreover, the habit of applying the term "subculture" primarily to what sociologists call "social problems" enhances the possibility that it will come to be associated only with disvalued things, much as the term "culture" has sometimes been taken to refer only to the strange customs of other peoples and not to our own way of life.

In the framework described here, the only kind of entity that can manifest a "subculture" is the *status class*—defined as a category of persons who share one or more socially recognized status characteristics that serve to differentiate them from other societal categories, and which serves as a basis for identification and allegiance. Perhaps the clearest example is found in those status classes based on sex or gender. There are two such classes, designated "male" and "female" on the basis of specific and differentiated biological characteristics. Once having defined these classes on the basis of criteria that are in large degree conceptually independent of forms of behavior one wishes to explain, one can proceed to delineate a large number of behavioral patterns and conceptions of appropriate practice manifested by persons by virtue of their affiliation with that class.

For example, those identified with the status class "males" maintain an intense and continuing interest and involvement in a set of activities centering around individual and collective competitive engagement—manifested in a thousand ways in organized athletics, warfare, business competition, scholarly debate, political rivalry, and so on. Because this consuming interest—what I have called a "focal concern"—is manifested in one of its myriad forms by all males whatever their age, social status, locality, or other bases of differentiation, it can be seen as a "property" of that particular class rather than of some other class. Similarly, those affiliated with the status class "females" maintain an intense and continuing interest in a wide range of enterprises centering on *mating and motherhood*—manifested in a thousand ways in family activities, preferred forms of fiction and drama, occupational preferences such as nursing and teaching, and many more.

These examples illustrate an important feature of the subcultural frame of reference. First, the concerns cited as characteristics of the two classes "males" and "females" are not *uniquely* or *exclusively* properties of that class. Females are also interested in competitive engagement—on one level through their involvement with male involvement therein, and on another level through their own. One might estimate that something on the order of 10 to 15% of females in the United States are consistent fans of big league baseball, compared to an estimate of 80 to 85% for males. Similarly, there are many males who manifest interest and concern with motherhood—both insofar as they are involved with female involvement therewith, and as a relatively independent concern.

But it is clear that the *kinds* of involvement of these two classes, as classes, are quite different. Motherhood engages most women with a degree of intensity that does not affect most men: competitive engagement plays a far more important part in the lives of most men than of most women. We are talking here about differences in the *scope or intensity* of involvement, and in the proportions of the total class that maintains high intensity interest. This is important because one of the most common criticisms of the subcultural approach is that it represents the behavioral patterns of different classes as completely distinct, separate, and mutually exclusive. In 1958 I referred to this phenomenon by writing that the focal concerns of a particular status class, "while by no means confined to the class at issue, represent a *pattern* of concerns which differs significantly, both in rank order and weighting, from that of other classes."[8] Some time later Oscar Lewis used these words:

> None of these traits [of the class] is distinctive per se; . . . it is their conjunction, their function, and their patterning that define the subculture . . ., that is, the distribution of the traits both singly and in combination will be greater [for a designated class] than in the rest of the population.[9]

The kinds of statements one makes on a subcultural level, then, are essentially *probability* statements, in the form "there is a 75% probability that 75% of those designated as 'male' or as 'middle class' or as 'adolescents' will manifest a particular interest or behavioral practice." Thus, when one attributes a particular characteristic to a particular status class, it generally indicates involvement by some substantial proportion of that class rather than all of it. Practices and concerns found in more than one class are generally differentiated by the *scope* and *intensity* of customary involvement, as in the case of parenthood as a concern of males and females. The various practices and concerns of a particular status class are also differentiated from those of other status classes in the degree to which they are related to *one another* (rather than to corresponding concerns of other classes) to form a distinctive pattern.

In order to specify as well as to limit the kinds of units to which one may attribute "subcultures," the present scheme delineates sixteen categories of status classes, organized around six principles of categoriza-

8  Walter B. Miller, "Lower Class Culture as a Generating Milieu of Gang Delinquency," *Journal of Social Issues*, XIV, No. 3 (1958), 6.

9  In Moynihan, *op. cit.*, p. 192. A brief version of this statement also appears in *The Children of Sanchez*, p. xxvii.

THE POOR

tion. These six are biology, geography-nationality, kinship, occupation, belief-ideology, and social station.
These are listed, along with the sixteen status-class
categories, in Chart I. The actual status classes delineated under each of these categories will not be
specified here, due to space limitations and because our
major concern is with "ranked position" classes.[10] In an
effort to specify greater and lesser degrees of influence
of status-class affiliation, the sixteen status-class categories are divided into two types, called "prime" and
"nonprime." "Prime" status-class categories are those
whose included classes encompass the total population
(as, for example, the two classes "male" and "female"),
and are limited in number, along with other defining
characteristics detailed in the expanded treatment.[11]

The five status-class categories designated as "prime"
under this system are those of *sex, age, residential
locale, region,* and *ranked social position.* Within each of
these a limited number of prime status classes are
delineated. Following Warner, the category "ranked
social position" includes the three conventional major
classes, upper, middle, and lower.[12] Within the lower
class, three subclasses, termed lower-class I, II, and III,
have been delineated, with "lower-class I" the highest
level. Defining criteria for each of these three levels have
been developed, but will not be detailed here due to
space limitations. Among terms commonly applied to
lower-class I is the "upper blue collar" or "stable
working class"; the term I generally apply to lower-class
III is the "low-skilled laboring class." This class is
defined primarily by its level of occupational involve-

[10] As an example, the major status classes included under the category
"residential locale" are, for general analytic purposes, urban, suburban,
and rural.

[11] W. B. Miller, "Subculture and Customary Behavior," p. 70.

[12] W. Lloyd Warner and Paul S. Lunt, *The Status System of a Modern
Community* (New Haven: Yale University Press, 1942).

# CHART I

Sixteen Status Class Categories

| *Categorization Principle* | | *Category* * | |
|---|---|---|---|
| I | Biology | 1. | *Sex* |
| | | 2. | *Age* |
| | | 3. | Physical Characteristic |
| II | Geography-Nationality | 1. | National Origin |
| | | 2. | *Region* |
| | | 3. | *Residential Locale* |
| III | Kinship | 1. | Relational Bond |
| | | 2. | Affiliational Unit |
| IV | Occupation | 1. | Vocation |
| | | 2. | Avocation |
| | | 3. | Habitual Pursuit |
| | | 4. | Education |
| V | Belief-Ideology | 1. | Religion |
| | | 2. | Politics |
| | | 3. | Special Cause |
| VI | Social Station | 1. | *Ranked Social Position* |

\* Prime status-class categories are *italicized.*

ment and customary forms of childrearing arrangements. Ten of its characteristics with respect to education, income, expenditure practices, and criminal behavior have been cited in a recent paper.[13]

One major problem in using the subcultural frame of reference concerns the actual process by which one's affiliation with various status classes affects one's involvement or lack of involvement in certain forms of

[13] W. B. Miller in Moynihan, *op. cit.,* pp. 260-262.

behavioral practice. If we take, for example, the customary behavioral practice—regular "informal" congregation at specific nonresidential locales—known as "hanging out" in many lower-class communities, it is obvious that this practice is more closely associated with the status class "male," "lower class," and "urban," and less closely with the classes "female," "middle class," and "rural." This problem is approached through the concept of *"subcultural conjunction."* Two orders of subculture are distinguished—"elemental" and "compound." An elemental subculture involves only one of the status classes previously described: a compound subculture more than one. Thus, the "female" subculture is elemental, "adolescent female" a double compound, "urban adolescent female" a triple compound, and so on. This conceptualization permits varying degrees of generality and specificity in designating customary practices, as well as serving a number of other conceptual purposes. For example, the actual nature of the "motherhood" focal concern, a property of the "elemental" female subculture because it is found among all sentient females regardless of their age, race, religion, social status, region, or other differences, can be characterized more specifically on the basis of subcultural conjunction; for example, it is manifested among female children (double compound status class) through involvement with baby dolls, and among older females in grandmotherhood.

The concept of subcultural conjunction may be applied quite usefully to reduce some of the conceptual confusion encountered by Lewis and others in handling the problem of variation in the subcultures of different kinds of low-status populations. One can move some distance in reducing this confusion, although not the whole distance, by cross-cutting the lower-class III subcultures to form sets of "double compound" subcultures. Thus, one has the male and female variants of low-status subcultures; the urban, suburban, and rural "residence-locality" variants; the southeastern, southwestern, and northeastern "regional" variants; the children's, adolescent, and adult "age-class" variants. Important as well are variants based on the nonprime categories of national origin and race; the white European, the Spanish-American, the American Indian, the African-American variants. By the same process one can become even more specific by delineating sets of triple or quadruple compounds—such as the subculture of low-status urban male adolescents—a category that figures prominently in many of the current problems of the central cities. The point here is that each of these sets of cross-cuts blocks out a set of variations of the "elemental" class-related subculture, which permits a far more refined set of statements than are possible on the basis of a notion of "the" culture of "poor" populations.

How does this outline of a rather elaborate scheme for subcultural analysis bear on the conceptual inadequacies of the "culture of poverty" concept? It shows, in the first place, that a major reason for dissatisfaction with the concept is precisely that it is *not* well enough elaborated. It is too global and undifferentiated. A sufficiently large number of the elements of Lewis' 70-trait model and its derivative listings simply do not apply, or apply inaccurately, to many of the various low-status populations that people are familiar with, in this country and elsewhere. The concepts of status class and subcultural conjunction make possible a systematic delineation of different kinds or types of variations of low-status populations on the basis of differences in age, in region, in urban-suburban-rural status, and the other cross-cutting status-class categories outlined here.

A second, and very serious defect, concerns the place or position of the Lewis' "culture of poverty" with respect to other cultures or subcultures. In the present approach the subcultures of low-status populations appear as one member, and only one member, of a *set* or *class* of analogous subcultures, to which it is systematically related. The subculture of low-skilled laboring populations appears in the context of two major dimensions—the ranked social strata dimension, where it shows important similarities to and differences from other ranked social strata such as the "blue collar" class, and the dimension of non-social-class subcultures, where it shows similarities to and differences from subcultures based on age, sex, locality, and so on. Comparative analysis within this latter dimension helps ascertain which of the elements of the subculture are attributable to low-social status as such: for example, the stress on stimulating experiences in the here and now, which is commonly seen as a characteristic of low-status subcultures, is also a property of the age-based subculture of adolescence, at all social status levels.

By failing to position his subculture in a systematic fashion with respect to the subcultures of other social status levels, Lewis denies himself a powerful analytic tool, and it is this failure that accounts in part for the accusations that the culture of poverty appears as a unique, isolated, and separate phenomenon, without meaningful ties to other parts of the society. While Lewis does cite other social classes occasionally, he does not present a systematic treatment of the relationship of the poverty subculture to the subcultures of other social strata, comparing it, instead, for the most part, to a gross entity called "the rest of society." A more adequate treatment along these lines might involve a set of cultures called the culture of affluence, the culture of near-affluence, of moderate wealth, of near-poverty, and so on, whose features could be compared systematically to those of the poverty culture.

However, as already suggested, I would see little

profit in such an approach, since I don't feel that the concept of "poverty" provides a good basis for a systematic treatment of subcultural differentiation. My objections are based, among other things, on dissatisfaction with an income-based criterion, with the use of a general condition such as "poverty" or "violence" to specify a class, and with the evaluative connotations of the concept. Lewis himself shares the notion that no single characteristic can adequately characterize a class-related subculture, so that the essence of a subculture lies in the complex network of *relationship* between its various component features. It is often useful, however, for communication and other purposes, to select one feature out of this complex by which to characterize the subculture as a whole, and we have found in our research that income is considerably less sensitive to status-related subcultural differences than other characteristics. The present use of the term "low-skilled laboring class" reflects our findings that occupational circumstances seem to play a more critical role in life style than income, and also that it is easier to see the logical connections between occupational involvement and other characteristics of any social class. As noted earlier, it is important, in the interests of minimizing tautology, to make the attempt to designate a specific population separately from the subculture it manifests. If one avoids the circularity of using the term "poverty" both to define the class and characterize its subculture and instead designates specific social strata on the basis of specific defining criteria, one can then treat the particular characteristics of low-status populations as manifestations of formal features found on *all* status levels. One can examine, for example, variations among the several classes in the forms and frequencies of elements such as educational attitudes and practices, income levels, recreational practices, prevalence and kinds of illegal pursuits, and so on.

115

A final conceptual defect concerns the "crucial element" aspect of Lewis' formulation. While Lewis has chosen to characterize his subculture by the term "poverty"—which is most commonly understood to mean having little money—he does not cite "low income" as the central feature of the subculture, but rather something having to do with "organization." Lewis never specifies very clearly what he means by organization, and in fact runs into quite a bit of trouble in trying to reconcile the apparently conflicting notions that slum communities rank low in "organization" yet at the same time contain units with a great deal of solidarity and a strong "sense of community,"[14] but he does make it quite clear that he regards as the crucial element of the subculture what he terms "non-participation in the major institutions of the larger society."[15] Putting aside the questions of what "major institutions" and "larger society" might mean (in the United States the numbers lottery is a major institution with probably more lower-class participants than there are middle-class participants in PTA's), Lewis suggests in several writings that if low-status populations somehow *do* become involved in the "major institutions of society" (which seem to mean in this context organizations that play some part in political decision-making processes), they no longer have a culture of poverty, even if the other sixty-nine traits of the subculture, including education, occupation, income, housing, and so on, have changed little.

The notion that a complex and multi-faceted subculture will no longer exist if one of its many elements is removed seems to indicate a bad misreading of the

[14] Compare the emphases in O. Lewis, *The Children of Sanchez,* p. xv, starting with "The sense of community is quite strong. . . ," with O. Lewis in *Scientific American, loc. cit.,* p. 22, starting with "the community . . . has a minimum of organization. . . ."

[15] *Scientific American, loc. cit.,* p. 21.

whole typological method of analysis, particularly as it applies to subcultures. It is not unlikely Lewis' choice of this criterion as "crucial" was motivated less by a concern with conceptual adequacy than by political and ideological considerations—an issue to be discussed next.

The second major deficiency in Lewis' "culture of poverty" concept, from the viewpoint of adequate understanding of low-status populations, concerns the role of what are very loosely called "values." I say "loosely" because there is no opportunity here to consider the multiple and diverse meanings of this term. "Values" will be used here in one of its many senses to refer in a very rough and imprecise way to those elements or aspects of social science formulations that attribute, either explicitly or implicitly, a greater degree of rightness or merit or worth or virtue to some of the objects under consideration and lesser degrees to others. The bases of these quasi-moral elements of evaluation may often be found in the normative definitions of one or more cultural or quasi-cultural systems. Among these are the subcultures of the various status classes (e.g., definitions of "bad" mothering practices in the female subculture), national cultures (e.g., goodness or badness of greater or lesser degrees of popular participation in the political process), theoretical or ideological frameworks of special belief or theoretical systems (e.g., value placed on "effective impulse control" or "sexual maturity" within the Freudian/psychodynamic theoretical system). It is obviously impossible to explore in any detail what all these systems are, and the kinds of evaluative standards associated with each. Instead, following paragraphs will simply cite, with no elaboration, some of the more obvious instances of special-system evaluation in Lewis' work as they are manifested in his choice of terms of reference.

These are grouped under four categories. The first might be called "simple derogation." Lewis characterizes males in the culture of poverty as "irresponsible," "generally unreliable," "immature," and "punishing," and female household heads as "authoritarian." The people in general are characterized as "ignorant" and "suspicious" and the culture in general as superficial and empty. Lewis says that his culture of poverty is "thin" and characterized by a "poverty of culture"—an odd phrase for an anthropologist to apply to a subcultural system with seventy traits.[16] The standards underlying these evaluations are derived from a variety of sources, and generally reflect widely held moral convictions of the general public.

The second category of evaluative terms is derived from what might be called "hidden reference standards"; that is, what appear to be semantically independent characterizations of the subculture or elements thereof actually involve a reference to or comparisons with another subculture or element, generally unspecified. Examples of this are found in the terms "marginal," "anachronistic," "underemployment," "early initiation into sex," "lack of privacy," "minimum organization," and "absence of childhood as a special age-stage."[17] The "hidden reference standard" component of each of these terms can be determined by applying to each the query: "With reference to what?"—for example, "lack of privacy," or "marginal," with reference to what? The hidden reference standard in such instances is sometimes, but not always, idealized practices of middle-class adult populations.

A third category consists of terms that derive their evaluative connotations from special assumptions about approved or desirable states or conditions as they are defined within particular analytic frames of reference or theoretical systems. Lewis' formulations are influenced

---

16 *La Vida*, p. lii.

17 *Ibid.*, pp. xlvii *passim.*

in particular, although not exclusively, by the definitions of mental or emotional health and ill-health of
psychodynamic theory. Lewis attributes to individuals
in the culture of poverty characteristics such as "high
maternal deprivation," "weak ego structure," and "confusion of sex identity."[18] From other special analytic
frameworks come the terms "alienated," "apathetic,"
and "imprisoned in a vicious cycle."

A fourth order of evaluative characterization is based
on speculative inferences as to subjective states of
individuals. Lewis attributes to persons in the culture of
poverty such characteristics as "strong feelings of
inferiority," "strong feelings of helplessness," "hatred
of the police," and a "pervading sense of hopelessness
and despair." Two major issues with respect to such
characterizations relate to the order of evidence upon
which they are based (interpretations of various kinds of
psychological tests employed by Lewis' researchers
embody the same kinds of assumptions as the parent
disciplines from which they are derived) and the issue of
insufficient specification. Do all people in the culture of
poverty hate all policemen at all times? Are all the
people hopeless and despairing under all circumstances,
at all ages, at all times?

A fifth category of evaluation is evidenced less by
specific terminology than by the general spirit or thrust
of the culture of poverty formulation as a whole. This is
the influence of the basic ideological assumptions and
related social-reform objectives of particular political
philosophies. Those aspects of Lewis' work and similar
writings influenced by shared and generally accepted
values of the national culture or of status-class subcultures do not ordinarily evoke particularly strong responses in the average American reader; those values
derived from particular partisan political philosophies,

---

[18] *Ibid.,* pp. xlviii *passim.*

on the other hand, have the capacity to evoke reactions of the most passionate sort. The rest of this paper will be devoted to this issue, since in my opinion the relationship between scholarly formulation and political values that figures so prominently in Lewis' writings reflects one of the most critical issues in social science today.

This issue, which may be phrased in crude and general terms as the relation of knowledge to values, is one of the oldest intellectual issues known, and has been a highly explicit concern in social science certainly since the beginnings of its "modern" phase—a period of roughly one hundred years. The issue has evoked brilliant and eloquent formulations by a host of scholars, including Karl Marx, Karl Mannheim, and Max Weber. All the arguments pro and con have been presented many many times, in great and elaborate detail, often with great force and cogency. It is quite impossible to say anything on this subject that has not been said before, and said extremely well. Why, then, raise the issue again at this particular time and under these particular circumstances? While the substance of the issue itself has changed very little over the years, it is my feeling that the *social context* within which it finds its expression has altered very significantly—particularly within the past ten years. How can one phrase this issue, hopefully in a fair and simple manner, in order to examine its current import? Again, crudely and at the risk of great oversimplification, it is possible to delineate two general positions with respect to the *objectives* of the scholarly enterprise of gathering knowledge with respect to social phenomena.

The first position is that the major and most immediate objective is to further the achievement of a good society and a good life for its members. Knowledge is viewed as an *instrument* for bringing about needed social reforms, and in particular eliminating a set of social ills such as war, poverty, injustice, inequality, bigotry, class discrimination, and racial prejudice. The validity of the enterprise as a whole is judged by the degree of success it achieves in producing concrete, specific, and workable methods for ameliorating social ills. The second position maintains that the major objective of the knowledge-gathering enterprise is to achieve as comprehensive, balanced, and accurate a picture as possible of the nature of social reality, and to develop descriptions and explanations of social phenomena that are influenced as little as possible either by the values of particular groups or by what are regarded at a particular point in time as social problems, or by the requirements of bringing about social reforms.

The two positions just outlined are phrased as "pure" or ideal polar positions, to emphasize their contrast. In practice, of course, there are many gradations between the two, and in theory, at least, a "central" position that effectively melds both objectives. Assigning names to these positions is even more risky than trying to characterize them briefly and fairly, but in the interests of conciseness the first might be called the "social relevance" position and the second the "pure knowledge" position. This issue is sometimes phrased as the opposition between "value-free" and "value-influenced" social science. I think this is an extremely misleading formulation, and that the notion of "value-free" or "detached and objective" scholarship is a straw horse. Few responsible scholars today deny the influence of values on knowledge. To be human is to value, and to engage in scholarly endeavor is to value mightily. Values of a hundred different kinds enter into our work at a hundred different points—in the selection of subjects to examine, in the choice of methods to pursue, in the gathering of data, in the analysis of findings, in the interpretation of results. The issue is not *whether* values influence social science formulations, but rather *which* values and *how much* and *to what ends.* For those who choose the "pure knowledge" alternative in one of its various forms, a more reasonable statement of purpose is to produce formulations that are as free *as possible* from the *unexamined* value premises of the various normative systems that affect one's work.

During the past half-century there has been, I believe, a fairly even balance between proponents of these two positions. Both sides command powerful arguments and have produced powerful champions. In my opinion this has been a good thing. Any strongly held "polar" position is prone to excess, and the persisting interplay and conflict between these two has served to limit and inhibit movement towards excesses inherent in both positions. The proponents of social relevance have kept the pure knowledge devotees from soaring too far aloft into the airy heights of arcane specialization; from indulging to access a preoccupation with picayune detail; from succumbing too far to the irresistible lure of the esoteric and the addictive fascination of abstract system-building. The "pure-knowledge" school has provided a leavening influence to the tendencies inherent in the social relevance position toward self-righteous dogmatism, the studied neglect of facts and views that cast doubt on the feasibility or desirability of particular reform objectives, the attribution of sacred infallibility to the premises of particular social or political theories. Until recently, in my opinion, this contest has been, by and large, a standoff, with beneficial consequences for both sides and the enterprise of knowledge-seeking as a whole. (The term "beneficial" reflects, of course, my own values.)

It is my impression that this balance has shifted markedly in the past decade—with "social relevance" gaining substantially at the expense of "pure knowledge." Both the reasons for this and its consequences are of considerable importance, but I will be able to touch on each only in the briefest manner. One frequently cited reason is the increasing participation of professionally trained social scientists in governmental policymaking, particularly at the federal level. This trend gained momentum in the 1930's with the movement of academic economists to Washington, and has now reached the point where many social scientists other than economists are actively involved in the formulation of governmental policies, not only as consultants, advisors and members of commissions, but as officials of the operating agencies themselves. Many of those who go to Washington come to relish the position of being close to the centers of power, and the understandable occupational concerns of those with direct responsibility for policy have produced many pressures—both direct and indirect—for the development of "policy-relevant" social-science formulations. These pressures, often originating with the most able men in the field, have diffused widely throughout the profession, with many consequences—not only in obvious ways such as the choice of areas for study and the sources of research financing, but in more subtle ways as well. There is increasing reliance, for example, on standards for judging the worth of a scholarly product that place greater weight on the ease with which it can be converted into programs of direct action and less weight on its empirical or conceptual adequacy.

A second reason, and one which engages us all at present, is related to the massive social reform movements that have swept the nation during the past decade. These center around the civil rights and anti-war movements, but have caught up in their wake a variety of related movements in such diverse areas as the participation of citizens in local government, the restructuring of the university, and the renewed thrust for women's rights. These social movements have had a powerful impact on the work of scholars in both direct and indirect ways. One of the most direct involves what might be called "market pressures." Most academic scholarship is conducted either in or under the influence of the university, and most scholars are in close contact with and highly sensitive to the actions and attitudes of college students—a group that is among the most active in the reform movements just noted. An intense desire to become deeply involved in a social or political cause is particularly characteristic of many of the present generation of students. Sensitivity to the concerns of this constituency has resulted in many efforts—some quite conscious, others less so—to tailor the academic product to fit the market demand. The market-like influences have affected not only the choice of subject matter for academic course offerings and the way in which courses are presented, but extend as well to the most basic levels of formulation—conceived by the professor with the student battle cry of "relevance" resounding in the background.

Related to these market demands are a set of pressures that exert a significant influence on the work of some scholars of the over-thirty generation. One group, men who played a major role in devising the intellectual formulations that undergird the present social movements, is gratified that their ideas have achieved such extensive currency and have had so marked an impact, and continue to play an active part both in leading and supporting the younger activists. A second group, men who made fewer contributions to these conceptual formulations, are nonetheless much concerned lest they appear to be following rather than leading the intellectual trends, and have become more royalist than the king, pressing the battle cries of "action" and "relevance" more fervently than the young activists themselves. It is my feeling that Lewis' work has been affected, in a more subtle fashion, by this latter tendency. A comparison of the general formula-

124

tions accompanying *The Children of Sanchez,* published in 1961, with those accompanying *La Vida,* published in 1968, shows a marked increase in particular ideological and political influences. For example, in 1961 Lewis wrote: "I want to draw attention to the fact that poverty in modern nations is not only . . . the absence of something; it is also something *positive*—a way of life [which is] remarkably stable and persistent."[19] His 1968 formulations, by contrast, emphasize the "lacks" and "absences" in his culture of poverty (recall the phrase "a poverty of culture")—the very tendency he decried seven years before.[20] The more recent formulations at the same time provide evidence of the increasing influence of ideologically derived evaluation, and represent an effort to play down the "remarkably stable and persistent" quality of the subculture so as to play up the feasibility of changing it through particular programs of social reform.

Given the present intellectual climate, it is of the utmost importance, in my view, to distinguish as clearly as possible between two separable issues. The first is: How *feasible* is the objective of developing a body of social knowledge that is as free as possible from unexamined values; and the second: How *free* should a scholar be to pursue this objective? The first issue, whether the quest for knowledge minimally influenced by values is either feasible or desirable, is infinitely arguable. The millions of words devoted to the question of feasibility attest to the fact that this subject is extraordinarily complex, since there are so many kinds and levels of "values" involved, and so many kinds and gradations of "influence." The issue of whether such an endeavor is even *desirable* is also highly complex, involving such factors as the unpredictable "practical"

19  *The Children of Sanchez,* p. xxiv.
20  In Moynihan, *op. cit.,* p. 189 *passim.*

125

uses of "pure" scientific research, the most economic utilization of limited knowledge-gathering resources, and many more. In all likelihood these issues will not be resolved for a long time to come, and in my opinion the continuing debate is a beneficial one.

As to the second issue, the freedom of scholars to pursue an ideal of "pure knowledge," my *own* values virtually dictate a strong and unqualified position. *Whatever* its feasibility, it is my firm conviction that scholars should be free, and should remain free, to pursue this objective if they so desire and can arrange supportive resources. This freedom is threatened, and dangerously threatened, in the present intellectual climate. The "pure knowledge" position has come to be considered—often by the most capable and perceptive proponents of social relevance—not merely as a rather harmless diversion to be regarded with amused tolerance, but in terms of the most active and passionate kind of moral condemnation—as an outrage, an abomination, an iniquity. For many of those to whom the terms "involvement," "action," and "relevance" have become the rallying cry of a great new movement towards a more just and a more humane society, the term "objective description" has become an acrid pejorative, and the words "pure knowledge" or "detached scholarship" or "scientific objectivity" are uttered only in tones of the bitterest sarcasm.

These shifts in the climate of permissible intellectual choice have affected every serious student of human behavior in society, impelling some mode of accommodation to the increasing pressures for social relevance. Again at the risk of severe oversimplification, three prevalent patterns of adaptation out of a wide variety of patterns may be cited. The first centers around the sentiment: "Why fight it?" Since we all recognize that all knowledge is heavily infused with values, that the advocacy of "pure knowledge" is either a delusion or a pious sham, that the claim to "scientific detachment" is a massive cop-out, and that any statement of relationship between parts of a society *is* a political statement—why be hypocritical? *Accept* the inevitability of values, and proceed openly and deliberately to gather, analyze, and interpret information in terms of particular social ideologies, political philosophies or social reform objectives. The writer of a recent book on poverty uses these words: "At least I am candid about my ideological orientation. Yes, my book *is* a 'dialectical argument.' "[21] I firmly uphold the freedom to adopt this stance, as I uphold the freedom to pursue "pure knowledge"—if, at the same time, the writer makes no claim of adherence to those canons of scholarship which call for balanced and comprehensive treatment, empirical and theoretical, but represents his work directly and openly as a partisan political document with partisan political aims.

A second pattern of adaptation involves a conflict—often a very serious one—for those scholars who experience at the same time a strong sense that social reforms are urgently needed and a desire to adhere to traditional canons of scholarship. This conflict appears with particular poignancy in the case of those anthropologists whose training was centered around the concept of culture—a concept represented to them as the keystone of the discipline, as its basic integrating principle, as the unique contribution of anthropology to social science. Such persons confront a serious dilemma. The concept of culture in one major formulation forwards a model of societal units whose various features are intimately related, mutually cohesive, "adaptive" in varying degrees to particular social and environmental conditions, and show, in consequence, a

21 Charles A. Valentine, "Reply to 'Culture and Poverty: Critique and Counter Proposals,' " *Current Anthropology,* X, No. 2-3 (April-June 1969), p. 197.

pronounced tendency to persist over time, and to resist in varying degrees particular kinds of social changes. This model (dismissed by some under the term "functionalism") is not, quite obviously, a congenial one for those to whom the ready or rapid achievement of social reform is a pressing objective. The movement toward a rejection of this anthropological tradition and its associated methods is manifest in extreme form in a current slogan, "To *describe* what *exists now* is to support the establishment," and in more extreme form in a companion slogan, "To *study* people at all is to exploit them." Evidence of this conflict emerges in the work of some of the most able and eminent anthropologists—wherein the whole concept of culture and its associated perspectives is called into serious question on the level of principle, but whose substance continues to show the powerful and pervasive influence of the concept. The resolution of the conflict in favor of social reform objectives is only apparent, and embodies a strong and persisting ambivalence.[22]

A third adaptation—probably the most common—involves the attempt to combine both kinds of objectives in the same enterprise—to produce work that is sufficiently careful, accurate, and internally consistent as to meet the requirements of scholarly adequacy, and at the same time sufficiently specific, problem-oriented, and policy-relevant as to meet the requirements of needed social reform. In my estimation this is the course Lewis has chosen, and the course in which he has failed. One brief example from his work will show how the two

[22] Among cultural anthropologists who have questioned the utility of the concept of culture as a valid basis of explanation for general and/or specific purposes are Elizabeth Jane Bott, *Family and Social Network* (London: Tavistock Publications, 1957), p. 218; Elliot Liebow, *Talley's Corner: A Study of Negro Streetcorner Men* (Boston: Little Brown, 1967), p. 208, and Liza Redfield Peattie, "Anthropology and the Search for Values," *The Journal of Applied Behavioral Science,* I, No. 4 (1965), 361-372.

objectives that have been treated separately here, conceptual adequacy and political orientation, affect one another, and how specific political values can affect both conceptual adequacy and logic. How can one account for Lewis' surprising suggestion that the culture of poverty does not exist in socialist countries? Recall that he makes a distinction between "poverty" and "the culture of poverty." He then selects as the "crucial element" in the "culture of poverty" something he calls "non-participation in the major institutions of the larger society." He next forwards the proposition that under socialism there *is* participation by the poor in the institutions of the larger society. Therefore, it follows directly, there can be no culture of poverty in socialist countries.[23]

The influence of political values on this logical argument seems obvious. Lewis' designation of "non-participation" as the "crucial element" in the culture of poverty rather than any of its many other characteristics clearly reflects a choice. One would expect, as already noted, that a subculture to which one assigns the term "poverty" would have "low-income" as its central element. Moreover, even the fact that Lewis takes the trouble at all to select one "critical element" seems to violate his own contention that it is a conjunction of many traits rather than any single trait which defines the subculture. These discrepancies, which are puzzling from the point of view of conceptual adequacy, become clear if one assumes that it is political orientation rather than logical adequacy that dictates the thrust of the argument.

Lewis' failure to combine two contrasting objectives raises the question of whether this mode of adaptation is possible. I would say that it is possible, in theory, but that the number of persons with the required capacities is negligible. To combine competent scholarship and

23 *La Vida,* p. xlix.

political relevance in a single work is not at all difficult, but to do it *well* is extremely difficult. The kinds of perspectives, the ways one organizes one's efforts, the ends one has in view, the audience one has in mind, in doing a creative and imaginative job of scholarly research are very different from those required to do a creative and imaginative job of policy formulation or implementation. H. Stuart Hughes, an academic historian who has performed with distinction in both roles, echoes Max Weber's classic 1918 essay in a recent speech: "There is an ethos, a professional standard, a pride and honor of the political man which is different from the ethos, the professional standard, the pride and honor of the intellectual. It is not impossible to perform well in both capacities, but it is difficult."[24] I share the conviction that the man who can perform with equally high quality both as scholar and policy formulator is rare indeed. At the same time I believe that the task of conceiving and executing imaginative and effective policies of directed social change is vital and urgent. How can both kinds of tasks be achieved? Not, as I have said, by an attempt to combine the two roles in a single person, but rather by maintaining a climate wherein *both* kinds of role—the activist, the reformer, the policy-innovator, *and* the scholar, the knowledge-seeker, the abstract-theory builder—are given the scope and freedom to do as well as they can that which each does best. It is always possible, where it does not happen naturally, to arrange modes of communication and contact whereby the concerns of the activist will inform the efforts of the scholar, and the formulations of the scholar facilitate the efforts of the activist. The purposes of social reform, however urgent, are poorly served over the long run by a social climate which degrades or devalues the worth of "pure knowledge."

---

[24] H. Stuart Hughes, "The Need Now is to Depoliticize the University," *Harvard Alumni Bulletin*, September 15, 1969, p. 36.

# COMMENTS ON "SUBCULTURE AND SOCIAL REFORM: THE CASE OF THE CULTURE OF POVERTY"

## ELLIOT LIEBOW

I shall not attempt a detailed consideration of Dr. Miller's paper but rather confine this discussion to a few general observations about some of his major points. At the outset I would like to express my grudging admiration for his expertise, and for the technical excellence and rigor and lucidity with which he presents his position, especially in regard to the subculture concept. And my admiration is grudging because, almost without exception, I find myself on the opposite side of the fence on every issue.

The matter of "pure knowledge" versus social relevance has, as Dr. Miller says, been the subject of millions of words. I will try to add as few as possible. I have 163 words on the subject.

First, I believe that social scientists along with everyone else must direct their efforts at somehow bringing under control those primitive forces that threaten our very existence. Now is the time for all good men to come to the aid of their party.

Second, I support Dr. Miller's plea that "scholars should be free to pursue 'pure knowledge' if they so desire and can arrange supportive resources." But if the scholar seeks such resources from public institutions, I hope his work is given low priority; I believe that the social science researcher, like everyone else, must justify his claim on public monies and support in terms of the likelihood of a substantial return to the public good. The argument that "you cannot tell beforehand, the serendipity factor you know" is a phony one. Of course, many things are logically possible but they are not equally possible. Given a scarcity of resources, we have to go along with what looks like the best bet in the light of current knowledge. And serendipity can smile on the researcher working on a social problem as well as on the man seeking "pure knowledge."

A final comment on a related point. Dr. Miller says that he firmly upholds the stance of the social scientist whose work is frankly and openly political on the condition that "the writer makes no claim to scholarly balance, or to empirical or theoretical adequacy." I do not understand this at all. To state one's biases, ideologies and politics openly and frankly would appear to be precisely the way to deal with those "unexamined value premises of the various normative systems which affect one's work." And whether or not a given piece of work meets the ordinary canons of science and scholarship seems to me to have nothing to do with why it was undertaken or what purposes it was designed to serve.

The delineation of five categories of inappropriate evaluative terms in Oscar Lewis' work left me unconvinced and uncomfortable. The important question is not whether Oscar Lewis or anyone else uses terms of evaluative characterization. "Authoritarianism," "alienation," "apathy," "lack of privacy," "strong feelings of inferiority," "hatred of the police," "pervading sense of despair"—these are all good words and phrases whose meanings are reasonably clear to all of us, and are not, in themselves, bad or wrong or inappropriate. The important question is whether the writer—in this case Lewis—provides sufficient evidence in support of these evaluative characterizations. In my opinion, Lewis does not—at least not in a form that readily enables the reader to match the evidence with the assertion—and it is this that is to be questioned, rather than the use of the terms themselves.

Although most of Dr. Miller's other criticisms of

Oscar Lewis seem well founded, his last reference to Lewis is not. He states that Lewis' designation of "non-participation" as the "crucial element" in the culture of poverty violates Lewis' own contention that it is a conjunction of many traits rather than any single trait which defines the subculture, and that this logical discrepancy becomes clear "if one assumes that it is political orientation rather than logical adequacy which dictates the thrust of the argument."

Concerning this point I suggest that Dr. Miller's own political orientation prevents him from seeing the logical possibility of a "critical element" in the constellation of subculture of poverty traits. For, as Dr. Miller notes, if one admits the logical possibility of a critical element ("non-participation" may not be a good name for it), and if this element is absent in socialist countries, then it is indeed possible for socialist countries to have bone-deep poverty unaccompanied by that social abomination labeled a "culture of poverty."

That part of Dr. Miller's paper in which he develops the concept of subculture is, I believe, a major contribution to the field. The analytically clear separation of the subcultures from their carriers, the status classes; the typing of the sixteen status-class categories into prime and nonprime; and most of all, the concept of subcultural conjunction, which permits the combination of single-element variants into compound wholes—all of these make possible a precision and rigor in the delineation and specification of subcultures and their variants that was not possible before. But one does pay a price for this precision. Using the four prime status-class categories appropriate to lower-class III (i.e., sex, residence-locality, region and age class) we get 54 variants of the lower-class III subculture alone. And if we add to this the crucial nonprime categories of race and national origin, we get 216 variants. Since even these categories must be refined further if we wish to distinguish between, say, Irish and Italian, or Puerto Rican and Mexican-American, each such refinement would add 54 to the number of logically possible variants of just the lower-class III subculture. In practice, of course, many of these logically possible variants would be ruled out, but the empirical determination of the character-istic features of even half that many subcultural variants would be an enormous undertaking and an especially difficult one in view of the accelerating rate of social change in the world we live in.

My own reservations about the subculture concept as presented here have less to do with its substance than with the usefulness of the concept for those whose primary interest is in social change. I was delighted with Dr. Miller's systematic delineation of the logical diffi-culties that inhere in the subculture concept and of the pitfalls that await its users. I found these so persuasive that, for one brief moment or two, I hoped he might himself be persuaded by his own argument.

Briefly and too simply, I think the subculture concept is more useful for describing human behavior than for explaining it. Dr. Miller, of course, would not agree with this. He says plainly at the outset that his purpose is to use the subculture concept to develop maximum explanational adequacy. From the perspec-tive of my own biases, I would argue that he provides us with a conceptual framework more suitable for purposes of description and classification than for explanation.

We are told, for example, that "The kinds of statements one makes on a subcultural level, then, are essentially *probability* statements, in the form—there is a 75% probability that 75% of those designated as 'male' or 'middle class' or as 'adolescents' will manifest a particular interest or behavioral practice." But, in themselves, probability statements or any other state-ments about what people do or are likely to do, however important, say little or nothing about *why* people behave as they do.

Let me make this point another way. In my own neighborhood of Brookland in Northeast Washington, long a racially mixed middle- to lower-middle-class neighborhood, there has been a recent influx of lower-class Negroes. Among the many changes that resulted was the transformation of the local Italian grocery store into a carry-out shop. We might explain this by saying that lower-class Negroes have a cultural aversion to Italian food, or that they have a cultural preference for the carry-out because it lends itself more easily to public socializing and hanging around, or simply that carry-out shops are characteristic of the lower-class Negro urban subculture.

Another change that resulted from the influx of lower-class Negroes was the conversion of detached, owner-occupied single-family homes into tenant-occupied multi-family dwelling units. And if you go into some of these houses, the conversion of the grocery store into a carry-out begins to take on a logic of its own. It seems to grow out of living arrangements, family structure, and work patterns rather than out of some vague assumptions about cultural preferences and life-style choices. The multi-family dwelling still has—as it did when it was a single-family house—only one kitchen, and the dining room has probably been converted into sleeping quarters. Moreover, many of the family units tend to consist of adult women and children, but whether the men are there or not, the women usually have jobs and are often unable to prepare meals and serve them even if they have the facilities to do so. This is not to say that lower-class Negroes do not buy groceries and eat at home. The point is rather that there are powerful political, economic, and social structural forces at work that tend to make family eating patterns among lower-class Negroes a more informal, more each-man-for-himself kind of thing than it is for their neighbors who are able to live in single-family houses. Hence the carry-out shop increasingly appears as a characteristic feature of the inner-city landscape.

It is presumptuous and dangerous, I believe, to view the prevalence of carry-outs and other lower-class patterns mainly as evidence of cultural choice. When we look at lower-class Negroes in cities, much of what we see is forced behavior rather than behavior of choice. In a very real sense, lower-class inner-city Negroes do not necessarily choose to eat in carry-outs any more than they choose to be poor, and it is being poor that often sets the life circumstances in which the carry-out and a host of other social forms and living patterns appear in the guise of cultural choice and life style.